AFRICA'S
PRIVATE SECTOR

AFRICA'S PRIVATE SECTOR

What's Wrong with the Business Environment and What to Do About It

Vijaya Ramachandran
Alan Gelb
Manju Kedia Shah

CENTER FOR GLOBAL DEVELOPMENT
Washington, D.C.

Library of Congress Cataloging-in-Publication data
Ramachandran, Vijaya.
    Africa's private sector : what's wrong with the business environment and what to do
about it / Vijaya Ramachandran, Alan Gelb, Manju Kedia Shah.
        p.   cm.
    Includes bibliographical references and index.
    ISBN 978-1-933286-28-0 (pbk. : alk. paper)
    1. Privatization-Africa.   2. Business enterprises-Africa.   I. Gelb, Alan H.   II. Shah,
Manju Kedia.   III. Title.
    HD4338.R36 2008
    338.96'05-dc22   2008044171

9 8 7 6 5 4 3 2 1

Printed on acid-free paper

Typeset in Minion and Univers Condensed

Composition by R. Lynn Rivenbark
Macon, Georgia

Printed by Versa Press
East Peoria, Illinois

Center
for Global
Development

The Center for Global Development is an independent, nonprofit policy research organization dedicated to reducing global poverty and inequality and to making globalization work for the poor. Through a combination of research and strategic outreach, the Center actively engages policymakers and the public to influence the policies of the United States, other rich countries, and such institutions as the World Bank, the IMF, and the World Trade Organization to improve the economic and social development prospects in poor countries. The Center's Board of Directors bears overall responsibility for the Center and includes distinguished leaders of non-governmental organizations, former officials, business executives, and some of the world's leading scholars of development. The Center receives advice on its research and policy programs from the Board and from an Advisory Committee that comprises respected development specialists and advocates.

The Center's president works with the Board, the Advisory Committee, and the Center's senior staff in setting the research and program priorities and approves all formal publications. The Center is supported by an initial significant financial contribution from Edward W. Scott Jr. and by funding from philanthropic foundations and other organizations.

Contents

Foreword

Gross domestic product in Africa has risen steadily over the past few years and is now growing at an annual rate of 6 percent. Economic growth in several non–oil exporting countries has also reached a robust annual rate of more than 5 percent, as those countries have seen significant improvement in the diversification and management of their economies. Macroeconomic reforms and improved political stability are producing significant results in terms of economic growth, and policymakers across the continent have better tools for combating inflation. Moreover, foreign direct investment in Africa has increased significantly since the early 1990s.

Yet there is much to be done, particularly in the area of *domestic* investment. In this book, Vijaya Ramachandran and her coauthors, Alan Gelb and Manju Kedia Shah, investigate the obstacles that Africans in the domestic private sector must deal with on a daily basis. Analyzing data from the World Bank's Enterprise Surveys, they argue that lack of infrastructure is one of the most serious constraints to the growth of Africa's private sector. In particular, the lack of a reliable supply of electricity significantly affects the productivity of businesses, especially those that cannot afford generators. The lack of a road network, resulting in the total absence of overland trade between Africa's two largest economies—Nigeria and South Africa—is also a serious problem. Finally, the authors argue that entrepreneurial capacity is constrained by the absence of broad-based, competing business networks, which further limits the ability of domestic investors to grow and thrive.

The authors present several solutions to these issues. One is that Africa has tremendous potential for the production of renewable energy: its reserves of renewable resources, including hydro, geothermal, wind, and solar power, are the largest in the world. There is scope for harvesting those resources, in both small- and large-scale projects. The authors make a strong argument that the time has come to make a real push toward helping Africa get on a carbon-free path to power generation by using the best available renewable energy technologies. And there is potential to address the transport bottleneck as well. A network of roads connecting all sub-Saharan capitals, along with the African Development Bank's proposed corridor network, would go a long way toward improving intra-African trade. And finally, investments in education, including nonformal methods of building entrepreneurial capacity and business networks, would help to create a broad-based private sector.

In 2003, I chaired the Commission on Capital Flows to Africa. We produced a report that argued that "increased capital flows can contribute significantly to Africa's development and that the U.S. government, together with the G-8 and OECD nations, could do much to stimulate and facilitate these flows." We said that the proposals in the report "would pay major dividends in terms of advancing U.S. humanitarian, foreign policy, and national security interests." Those statements are perhaps even more relevant today. Given the current global turmoil and the headwinds that the continent is likely to face going forward, the conclusions in this book are all the more important. A strong, vibrant private sector in Africa is central to creating jobs and economic growth in the region, and it also will create demand for goods and services from countries around the world.

JAMES A. HARMON
Chairman
Caravel Management

New York
December 2008

Preface

At the Center for Global Development, we are concerned primarily with rich-world policies on aid, trade, and other issues that shape the chances for poor countries and poor people to improve their well-being. Among regions, Africa has the largest number of countries that are highly dependent on aid, and from our inception seven years ago, we have worked on reform of the donor aid system and on debt relief programs that matter immensely for Africa. However, the reality is that sustainable growth in Africa depends less on aid than on global and domestic policies and investments that support the creation of businesses and job growth.

As this book goes to press, growth rates in the developing world—and the reductions in poverty that accompany growth—are at risk due to a global financial crisis and economic downturn that began in the United States. The prospect of a global recession raises the question of whether Africa's growth, at an average annual rate of between 3 and 5 percent over the past five years, is adequately rooted in a thriving domestic private sector or whether it is instead the outcome of external factors, including the commodity boom driven by growth elsewhere (such as in China) and the increase in foreign private inflows helped along until late 2008 by low global interest rates.

Vijaya Ramachandran and her coauthors address that question and many others as well: Can African firms compete against the Chinese manufacturing juggernaut? How do government regulations and the lack of infrastructure affect their costs and competitiveness? How well do local financial markets provide credit, especially to indigenous firms?

Using carefully gathered and unusually thorough survey data, the authors describe the state of small businesses and the obstacles facing them, and they point policymakers toward the investments in infrastructure and education that would help unlock the vast potential of the African people. The authors' investment in practical evidence shines in their careful approach to its analysis, which comes to life through the many examples of the difficulties that businesspeople in Africa face. A firm in the Democratic Republic of Congo must resort to airlifting cement to avoid poor roads. Manufacturers in Kenya have been asked to operate at night to reduce the load on an overburdened electrical grid.

Finally, the authors show that sparse and fractured markets in Africa make trade less profitable and economies of scale more difficult to achieve. In this already difficult business environment, large indigenously owned firms are few in number and lag behind their non-indigenous counterparts. Supporting indigenous firms must be a focus of policymakers in order to create a broad-based private sector.

Jim Harmon's foreword calls attention to the implication of this work for the global community, including the incoming administration in the United States. Indeed, the analysis in this book expands on the policy recommendations in CGD's *The White House and the World: A Global Development Agenda for the Next U.S. President,* and it also builds on our earlier work on the future direction of the African Development Bank.

The work that led to this book is part of the Center's portfolio of policy research on weak and fragile states, which benefits from the financial support of the Australian Agency for International Development. We also are very grateful to our board member, James Harmon, for his support of this work and for his deep commitment to development and poverty alleviation in Africa. Finally, we thank Edward Scott Jr., the chairman of our board, for his ongoing support of the Center's work.

Nancy Birdsall
*President
Center for Global Development*

*Washington, D.C.
December 2008*

Acknowledgments

We are grateful to several people for sharing their knowledge, insights, and expertise on the issue of private sector development in Africa. Nancy Birdsall gave us sound advice and encouragement throughout the writing process. Dennis de Tray, Kim Elliott, Enrique Rueda-Sabater, Ted Moran, Todd Moss, Phil Keefer, Gaiv Tata, George Clarke, Arvind Subramanian, David Wheeler, Michael Clemens, Steve Radelet, and David Roodman provided valuable comments and suggestions. George Clarke, Jorge Rodriguez-Meza, and Alvaro Gonzalez generously helped us with the sampling methodology and the use of the Enterprise Surveys database. Benn Eifert coauthored earlier work on enterprise productivity and provided valuable insights on various parts of the analysis. Robert Bates reviewed the manuscript and provided us with very helpful comments.

We also gained many insights from presenting various parts of this book to audiences of policymakers, academics, and private sector businesspeople at the University of Cape Town; the African Development Bank; the Private Investors for Africa Group; the Africa Advisory Council of Heineken N.V.; Georgetown University; Cornell University; the South African Economics Association; the World Bank Annual Conference in Development Economics (in Dakar); the Millennium Challenge Corporation; the Development Economics Research Group of the World Bank; the Trade, Aid and Security Coalition; the Society for International Development; and the National Bureau of Economic Research. In particular, we would like to thank Dave Kaplan, Alan

Hirsch, Olu Ajakaiye, Benno Ndulu, John Nellis, Marilou Uy, Peter Timmer, Demba Ba, Melanie Mbuyi, Giuseppe Iarossi, Jean Michel Marchat, Ivan Rossignol, Jim Emery, Michael Klein, Guy Pfeffermann, Devesh Kapur, John Nellis, James Habyarimana, Mary Hallward-Driemeier, Taye Mengistae, Ritva Reinikka, Jeri Jensen, and Nicolas van de Walle.

Sina Grasmann, Nicole Smalls, and Sarah Rose provided excellent research assistance, as did Robin Kraft, who went above and beyond the call of duty in getting this manuscript ready for publication. Lindsay Morgan and John Osterman guided the manuscript through publication. We are grateful for their help.

This analysis is based on surveys of thousands of African businesspeople who are trying to keep their businesses running despite all sorts of obstacles. We are deeply grateful to them for their time and effort, and we hope that the solutions proposed in this book will be of use to them. We are thankful as well for support from the Australian Agency for International Development, which has helped make this work possible.

Summary

The performance of Africa's economies has improved recently, but there is still a huge lag in terms of long-term growth, structural change, and industrial development. Why is business performance lagging in Africa? And is Africa different from the rest of the developing world?

This analysis brings together a number of issues emerging from Enterprise Surveys that have been conducted in several countries in sub-Saharan Africa and elsewhere. It does not cover all of the many causes that have been proposed to explain the slow rate of growth in Africa. It concentrates instead on what managers and entrepreneurs in the private sector in Africa are telling us about the day-to-day problems that they encounter. The analysis in this book is a reflection of their point of view. The businesses that they run are located in the formal manufacturing sector, which, even though it is not the dominant sector of economic activity, is vital in the chain of development.

Our central thesis is that the observed lags in the development of the private sector in Africa are based on the interaction of several factors:

Exogenous factors. These include the small size of markets and overall economic sparseness, which together discourage competition and innovation, reduce the entry of new firms, and increase demands on infrastructure.

Infrastructure. The lack of infrastructure, particularly a reliable source of power, emerges as a huge constraint on private sector activity. More than half of all private sector firms rank infrastructure as their worst constraint. Firms that are able to compensate for lack of electricity by using generators are able to survive better than firms that do not have a generator. Furthermore, the low density of economic activity raises demands on infrastructure.

Segmented business sectors. Many African countries have private sectors that are ethnically segmented or dominated by ethnic minorities or both; these segmented networks exist for reasons of history, adaptation to risk, and so forth. Segmented networks in already sparse economic environments limit competition, encourage an ambivalent attitude toward facilitating a good business environment, and constrain the growth of firms outside the dominant network. Large markets may compensate for ethnic segmentation by encouraging entry or sustaining multiple networks, but that is not the case in much of Africa. We have yet to see the emergence of a broad-based business class.

While the economic fundamentals are in place in many African economies, there is no central authority to make critically needed regional investments—no equivalent of a federal government or a pan-African highway administration or power authority with a mandate to fill the gaps in regional investments. Internal markets remain small and segmented, exporters face high costs of transportation, and key bottlenecks to growth are not alleviated.

What does all of this mean for the development of Africa's private sector? Several reforms are potentially important and can reinforce each other:

—Open borders, which encourage conglomeration, increase the scale of markets and the density of economic activity.

—Improvements in key infrastructure constraints, especially power and roads.

—Introduction of service guarantees to improve the responsiveness of governments to the service needs of businesses.

—Efforts to broaden the base of the private sector, through the strengthening of private-public dialogue and support of home-grown efforts such as the Investment Climate Facility for Africa.

Finally, what can rich countries do to help with the agenda above? There is scope for both bilateral and multilateral assistance in all four areas, particularly in the area of infrastructure investment. The Overseas Private Investment Corporation (OPIC) in the United States and other organizations should set up funds to support "clean infrastructure" projects that focus on renewable energy sources. Newly emerging economies such as China and India, as well as the United States and other rich countries, can help to shape the African Development Bank's portfolio, so that it can focus on the financing and implementation of infrastructure projects. Rich countries also can do more to facilitate the transfer of renewable energy technologies to Africa.

Entities that offer investment guarantees can expand their coverage to domestic investors by introducing partial risk guarantees. Both rich countries and multilateral banks can help African governments move toward creating more open borders and a less onerous regulatory environment by supporting the newly created Investment Climate Facility for Africa. And both can provide assistance for programs, particularly in the area of business education, that will help small entrepreneurs become more successful.

Introduction
Africa's Private Sector

In the summer of 2007, the government of Kenya made an urgent appeal to the Kenya Association of Manufacturers. It asked the members of the association to move their production schedule from their usual hours to a nighttime schedule of 11:00 p.m. to 5:00 a.m. The reason was that Kenya was running out of electricity and was unable to provide power for more than a few hours a day; massive load shedding was required so that the power system would not be overwhelmed. The association acknowledged the problem but wondered how workers would get to and from work in the dark and what sorts of logistical and security costs would be incurred. Kenyan firms already were paying about 4 percent of sales in security costs to keep their workers and equipment safe.

The same summer, President Museveni of Uganda decided to grant 7,100 hectares of Mabira Forest to the Mehta Group, an Asian-owned conglomerate that intended to use the land to grow sugarcane. He explained in a letter to members of parliament that Asian entrepreneurs were crucial to the success of the Ugandan economy and should be given every opportunity to generate jobs for the Ugandan people. But many were not convinced. The immediate reaction was violent rioting, which, according to media reports, resulted in at least two deaths. The opposition Forum for Democratic Change accused Museveni of favoring Asians and pointed out that doing so could lead to racial tensions. Several commentaries in the Ugandan media argued that Mabira Forest was an environmentally sensitive area that deserved to be protected, not destroyed by sugarcane cultivation. The Asian community and the Kampala City Traders Association went to some lengths to assure everyone that their relationship was intact and that the association included several thousand Asian members. Ultimately, President Museveni backed down. But the situation has served to highlight the issue of ethnic minority dominance of the formal private sector—a contentious issue in many African countries.

These are two examples of the key issues affecting the performance and structure of Africa's formal manufacturing sector, which is the topic of this book. Manufacturing constitutes only a modest part of Africa's economies, and generally it has not been their most dynamic sector. Why, then, focus on it in this way? We offer three reasons. First, one of the characteristics of most fast-growing developing countries has been their ability to evolve structurally—away from the primary sector (agriculture) and toward a more diversified mix of the primary, manufacturing, and service sectors—and to move up the technology ladder. While currently high commodity prices may be helping to sustain growth in many African countries, it is likely that without such a structural transformation, their growth will continue to be sporadic and to lag behind that of other countries.

Second, in Africa and other developing regions there has been more extensive study of the manufacturing sector's performance and its links to the business climate than of that of other sectors, such as services and tourism. While some of the factors affecting manufacturing may be specific to the manufacturing sector, many obstacles, whether related to infrastructure or governance and other regulatory factors, will apply to a wider range of formal activity. Third, a look at the structure and makeup of the manufacturing sector can throw light on some of the political economy factors that influence the speed at which countries are ready to implement deep business climate reforms.

Moving forward, perhaps the most important determinant of performance will be the business environment in which firms operate. Does it encourage firms to learn, to invest and grow, and to compete on a global scale? Or does it involve high costs and risks that create disincentives for an entrepreneur who might wish to establish a business, invest in it, or increase its productivity? Is the business environment competitive enough to spur innovation and expansion, or does it impede change?

Particularly in Africa, however, we cannot consider performance without considering "agency"—the capabilities and capacities of the firms themselves, of their entrepreneurs and managers. Are these agents able to take advantage of the opportunities offered by an increasingly open and globalizing Africa? If so, which kinds of owners, managers, and entrepreneurs have more access to opportunities and which have less? Are there major differences, in particular between indigenous firms and foreign- or minority-owned businesses? If so, what might that mean for the political economy of business-government relations?

That brings us to our discussion of policy solutions. A key question is how to strengthen support for expanding opportunities and the political economy of pro-business reforms. What factors encourage governments to provide essential infrastructure and regulatory services to businesses and to move aggressively to improve the business climate? Is the business community likely to push this agenda, or is it more likely to stand on the sidelines or even to resist reforms? Are the gains from reforms seen as sufficiently attractive to offset the risks, including greater competition? And how are the trade-offs affected by the structure and makeup of the business sector and the size of the market in which it operates?

In focusing on these three topics we concentrate on low-income countries in Africa that have progressed substantially in first-generation macroeconomic reforms. Much of the analysis draws on firm surveys conducted across many African countries between 2001 and the present. Chapter 1 presents an overview of Africa's economies, including data on GDP, economic density, and the manufacturing sector. Africa is distinctive in several ways—in particular, economies are both very small and very sparse, and their manufacturing sectors are modest. These structural factors have several implications for industrial structure and performance, through factors such as the cost of providing infrastructure and the potential for competition.

Chapter 2 presents findings indicating that firms in many African countries bear a heavy burden of indirect costs and losses that make their overall profitability lower than might be expected on the basis of their factory-floor productivity. These findings suggest that despite frequently low productivity and serious skill deficiencies, unit labor costs may not be the binding constraint on firms in Africa. Many of Africa's firms are quite productive, and the question often is how to bring down indirect costs and losses to enable higher-value-added production and generate profits to feed into investment, fund growing, and higher pay for the workforce. In addition to providing quantitative evidence in firm surveys, firms also are providing useful qualitative feedback on the perceived severity of different constraints. The relative importance that firms place on physical infrastructure (in particular the cost and reliability of power supplies), finance, governance, regulation, and services can be of great use to policymakers who must decide what priority to give various interventions to improve the business environment.

Chapter 3 turns to another set of key issues—the patterns of ownership and capabilities in different groups of firms in African countries. Productivity analyses suggest that, in addition to the dampening effects of a poor business environment on all firms, many countries confront considerable segmentation between larger and smaller businesses and between more and less productive businesses. That segmentation often is related in a pronounced way with whether a business owner is domestic or foreign and with the ethnicity of the owner. The question is not why there are so few "black-owned" businesses. In all countries there are many such firms and indeed many highly successful ones that increasingly are investing outside their own countries. However, it is also often the case that bigger businesses, more productive firms, and export firms are still largely foreign owned or owned by ethnic minorities, whether Asian, Middle Eastern, or Caucasian. Why that is so is a complex question with a variety of explanations, including colonial history, the political and economic management of a country since colonialism, differential access to information and finance, and possibly commercial culture. Our data show, for example, that indigenous firms tend to start smaller and grow more slowly than minority-owned businesses and that different factors seem to influence their growth. We explore the reasons for this phenomenon in the broader context of the political economy of the private sector in Africa.

Why have low-income economies in Africa not undertaken more aggressive reforms? Certainly there are some notable successes, most recently, for example, in Rwanda, where the government has undertaken a series of reforms to improve the business environment. Yet business climate indicators reported in the World Bank's *Doing Business* rankings still lag in many African countries.[1] Some observers have noted a degree of ambivalence toward the market-based model of economic development in Africa and less follow-up on macroeconomic and trade reforms, which, in any event, are widely seen as having been imposed during the structural adjustment period rather than having resulted from countries' own efforts to secure access to markets abroad.[2] We consider some political economy explanations in chapter 4, including the implications for small countries of having sparse, fragmented business communities in which the indigenous sector is lagging.

These three issues—costs, the structure of the business community, and the process of reforming the business environment—are seen as interrelated. Without stronger business communities, including indigenous constituen-

1. World Bank (2001–07).
2. World Bank (2000).

cies, support for better business services and more stable and predictable policies will continue to be weak. At the same time, the creation of an effective lobby for broad pro-business reforms is constrained by unresponsive policies and poor implementation. *The central question is why the structure of the business environment looks the way it does.* What are the underlying factors constraining the performance of firms, and what policies will help address them?

Chapter 4 draws on the above analysis to suggest ways to encourage investment, focusing on solutions that have emerged from within Africa. There is no single binding constraint and no "silver bullet" to eliminate it, but the research and data that are becoming available on Africa's firms and business climate can help increase the possibility of accelerating regulatory and institutional reforms to complement improvements in infrastructure and macroeconomic management. We look for specific approaches to private sector development that we believe will make a difference for growth in the African private sector. Although the better information on the quality of regulation and business services now becoming available can be a powerful tool for accelerating reforms, that information needs to be integrated more systematically with reforms in other key areas of the business environment and into a structured dialogue between governments and private sector groups.

one

The Countries and the Surveys

Over the last decade, Africa's economic performance has improved markedly. Gross domestic product per capita has risen since 1994, relieving some of the pessimism about the future that had been so prevalent before. No longer is Africa seen as a "Hopeless Continent."[1] Oil exporters have been boosted by large terms-of-trade gains, and with better macroeconomic management, an opening to trade, and increased private sector activity, some eleven low-income countries (which are not exporters of oil) have been growing at an average rate of 5 percent, reversing the twenty-five-year trend of falling real incomes and rising poverty (Gelb, Ramachandran, and Turner 2007). Foreign direct investment (FDI) in many of these countries has expanded fourfold since the early 1990s and has begun to diversify, including investments in a widening range of goods and services as well as traditional investments in natural resources. Moreover, the sources of FDI have diversified. While South Africa was the initial source of most such investment, sources today increasingly include Asian countries.

These favorable economic trends have developed in a generally improving political context. While there have been notable setbacks, many former autocracies have moved toward multi-party elections, with indicators of civil rights and political liberties showing substantial gains since the early 1990s, partic-

---

1. "Hopeless Africa," *Economist*, May 11, 2000.

6

ularly in the better-performing countries (Radelet 2008). While not always fully free or fair, elections have provided an opportunity for local voices to be heard and, in some cases, for greater accountability of governments and stronger pressure on governments for more effective service delivery. Several countries have seen peaceful transitions of government, in some cases more than once. Seen in the context of new states—and considering the experience of Latin America in the last century or the trials of Indonesia, now generally considered a relatively successful case of development during its nation-building period—Africa's political trajectory is perhaps not as exceptional as often supposed.

These factors augur well for Africa's future. Yet there is still concern over the sustainability of Africa's economic gains, over the fact that they have not been shared by all countries, and over the possibility that at least part of the improved performance has been encouraged by exceptionally favorable trends in terms of trade. Unlike the rapidly growing Asian economies, whose rising incomes have been associated with structural shifts from agriculture to industry, even the better-performing low-income African economies have tended to move from agriculture toward the tertiary sector, with relatively slow growth in industry and sluggish industrial employment growth (figure 1-1). In addition, total investment has often grown less than might be expected given the substantial gains in FDI, suggesting that domestic processes of accumulation and investment are still weak (Gelb, Ramachandran, and Turner 2007). Moreover, because of low incomes in Africa, the gap with other regions continues to widen in absolute terms even if there is a slow convergence in percentage terms. This is very different from the picture in China and other countries in Asia, where rapid growth and penetration of world markets with manufactured exports are driving the economic and social transformation of those countries.

Central to the issue of growth in Africa is the viability and vigor of its private sector. Increased productivity is the driving factor of economic growth—without it, there is no real chance for Africans to raise their standard of living and quality of life. The private sector generates jobs and incomes and sustains a middle class, which leads in turn to an increase in political accountability and the strengthening of democratic institutions and processes. Many factors can underlie global differences in productivity, not all of them well understood. They can include, for example, demographics, human capital effects, spatial factors associated with neighborhood effects, or technological breakthroughs, such as the Green Revolution, that favor one type of physical

Figure 1-1. Sector Shares of GDP in Africa, 1990 and 2005

Percentage of GDP

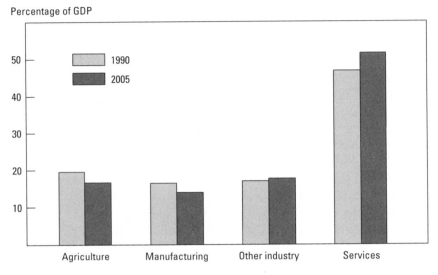

Source: World Bank (2007).

environment over another. This book does not seek to be an exhaustive study of all possible causes; it focuses instead on a set of factors related to the business environment in Africa.

Before we move to our analysis, let us take a quick look at the twenty-nine African countries covered in this book. Table 1-1 describes the gross domestic product per capita of the countries in the sample. The first point to note is the very small size of African economies. At barely $3 billion, the median economy is a fraction the size of any of the comparator economies. With the exception of a few middle-income countries, almost all have a per capita GDP of less than $500 a year. The data on economic density provide additional perspective. Most African countries are very sparsely populated in comparison with India, China, and Indonesia. Of the twenty-seven countries, only seven have more than 100 people per square kilometer. Many are well below fifty people per square kilometer—a density that is one-seventh that of India and one-third that of China. The combination of low population density and low incomes compounds economic sparseness. Africa's GDP per square kilometer is far below that of China, India, Indonesia, and the United States. With the exception of Mauritius (a real outlier), South Africa, Cape Verde, and (marginally) Rwanda, every country produces less than $100,000 per square kilometer. Some countries are in the range of $10,000 to $20,000. Nine countries—the Democratic Republic of Congo, Guinea-Bissau, Madagascar, Mali, Mauritania, Mozambique, Namibia, Niger, and Zambia, produce less than $10,000 per square kilometer, and some are relatively large. It is interesting to note that some of these countries have had high growth rates in the past. Nonetheless, sparseness of population has led to a low spatial density of economic activity in comparison with density in India and China, which is more than $200,000 per square kilometer in both.

Road density also is very low in Africa relative to density elsewhere. Most African countries have less than 10 kilometers of roads per 100 square kilometers of land, while there are 20 kilometers of roads in China, 70 kilometers in the United States, and 113 kilometers in very dense India. Equally relevant is another measure of economic density, GDP per kilometer of road. Most countries in Africa produce less than $1,000 per kilometer of road, while the figure is about $18,000 per kilometer in the United States and $11,000 in China. This sparseness suggests the difficulty of connecting producers and consumers in Africa, as well as the costs of maintaining roads and utilities relative to available resources.

Table 1-1 also describes the share of the manufacturing sector in GDP and the importance of manufactured exports as a share of total exports. Manufacturing as a share of total economic activity, which is about 30 percent in China and Indonesia, is still relatively low in most African countries, around 10 to 20 percent of total GDP. Manufactured exports as a share of total exports is high for a few countries—Senegal, South Africa, Mauritius, Swaziland, and Mali—but in most cases their exports represent early-stage processed primary products, and the share is low elsewhere. In contrast, diversified manufactures comprise a large part of comparators' exports.

Africa's low population density and low level of education suggest that it is resource rich and skills poor. A cross-country study by Wood and Mayer (1998) confirms that assessment and also suggests that such factor proportions are strongly associated with a primary products-based export structure. However, traditional comparative advantage based on factor proportions does not provide a complete explanation of Africa's low income level, its dynamic path of factor accumulation (which has been fraught with the flight of financial and human capital, despite the assumption that both are "scarce" factors), or the fact that wages are lower in some African countries than in manufacturing powerhouses like China, which often are assumed to compete on the basis of cheap labor. Factor endowments are not the only driver

Table 1-1. Economic Density and Exports in Africa

Country	GDP[a] (PPP in billions of dollars)	2005 GDP per capita[a] (PPP in dollars)	Population density[a] (people per square kilometer)	GDP per square kilometer[a] ($1,000s)	Road density[a] (kilometers of road per 100 square kilometers)	GDP per kilometer of road ($10,000s)	Percentage of manufactures in total exports	Adult literacy
Angola	33.1	2,077	13	27	4.1	64	...	67
Benin	8.6	1,015	76	77	17.2	45	6.8	35
Botswana	19.5	11,021	3	34	4.3	80	71.2[b]	81
Burkina Faso	14.3	1,079	48	52	5.6	93	14.7[c]	22
Burundi	4.7	622	294	183	48.0	38	3.9	59
Cameroon	33.4	2,045	35	72	10.7	67	2.6[d]	68
Cape Verde	2.6	5,162	126	649	33.5	194[e]	8.8[f]	...
Congo DR	36.6	635	25	16	6.8	24	...	67
Gambia, The	2.6	1,709	152	259	37.4	69	7.6[f]	...
Guinea	19.4	2,060	38	79	18.1	44[b]	22.4[g]	29
Guinea-Bissau	1.2	736	56	42	12.3	34[g]	...	...
Kenya	37.8	1,103	60	66	11.1	60	16.3[d]	74
Lesotho	5.3	2,967	59	175	19.6	90[h]	79.6[g]	82
Madagascar	15.3	821	32	26	8.6	31[h]	29.5	71
Malawi	7.6	593	137	81	16.4	49[b]	10.6[g]	64
Mali	12.4	919	11	10	1.5	66	8.3[d]	19
Mauritania	6.1	1,988	3	6	0.8	80[h]	...	51

Mauritius	14.1	11,312	612	6,928	99.3	698	35.8	84
Mozambique	21.9	1,105	25	28	3.9	72[h]	4.3[f]	..
Namibia	13.7	6,749	2	17	5.1	32[g]	45.7	85
Niger	9.7	695	11	8	1.2	67	12.3	29
Nigeria	131.9	1,003	144	145	21.0	68[d]	2[b]	..
Rwanda	9.7	1,073	366	393	56.8	69	4.7[b]	65
Senegal	18.6	1,594	61	97	7.1	137[b]	26.7[d]	39
South Africa	463.5	9,884	39	382	30.0	127[c]	47.1	82
Swaziland	4.9	4,292	66	282	20.9	135[g]	64.5	80
Tanzania	25.4	662	43	29	8.9	32[b]	8	69
Uganda	37.3	1,293	146	189	35.9	53[b]	7.3	67
Zambia	10.6	910	16	14	12.3	12[c]	7.8	68
China	7,842.2	6,072	140	841	20.1	406	84.4[f]	91
India	3,362.1	3,072	368	1,131	76.8	99[g]	45.5	61
Indonesia	754.1	3,419	122	416	20.3	205[g]	40.2[e]	90
United States	11,046.4	37,267	32	1,206	70.2	172	56.2[f]	..

Source: World Bank (2007).

a = data from 2005.
b = data from 2003.
c = data from 2001.
d = data from 2004.
e = data from 2000.
f = data from 2006.
g = data from 2002.
h = data from 1999.

of costs and factor prices. Two other theories, ably surveyed by Burgess and Venables (2004), suggest other critical factors.

The first theory stresses an economy's ability to provide non-traded producer goods and services to underpin secondary sectors that typically are more "transaction-intensive" than the primary products and subsistence agriculture sectors (Collier 2000). Various problems, such as poor business services, including macroeconomic management and governance; policy instability; and inadequate infrastructure, regulation, security, and logistics, create high costs and high risks (Moss 2007). They squeeze out potential investments across a wide range of sectors that include not only manufacturing but also resource processing and tourism. The second theory (Krugman 1980, 1991a, 1991b) stresses producer externalities and learning created by "thick" markets and a critical mass of producers. Both theories are highly relevant for Africa's very small and very sparse economies. The small GDP of the median country is likely to reduce the incentives for new entry and to limit innovative pressure due to domestic competition. The sparseness of Africa's economies means that there are few significant industrial clusters. Kenya's horticulture-floriculture complex offers one example; another is Madagascar's zones for processing textile and garment exports. There are some signs of "thickening," including through developing tourism circuits, mostly in the south and east of the continent. But relative to business in other regions, business in Africa is sparse and has a relatively low connectivity.

This discussion leads to a question—is Africa "different" from other developing regions? The question is difficult to answer, but the data presented above point us toward some of the differences that can be investigated using Enterprise Survey data—notably the high cost of doing business and the interaction between low economic density and the political economy of regulation.

The Surveys and Data

Before proceeding any further, we want to say a few words about our data. The analysis presented in this book is based largely on the World Bank's database of Enterprise Surveys. These are door-to-door surveys of businesses, and they cover the manufacturing sector as well as other sectors such as services, tourism, and so forth. The survey data reflect the views of the business sector itself—how businesses view their own environment. This is a unique perspective and one not often found in the literature on Africa's growth, much of which relies on macroeconomic data or secondary sources of information.

The surveys, which were conducted between 2001 and 2008, cover a stratified, random sample of firms in each country. They focus on the measurement of enterprise-level productivity and the characteristics of the investment climate in which the firms operate.[2] A standardized core questionnaire was used in all countries, enabling benchmarking of the crucial variables of investment, employment growth, and productivity for firms in the formal sector. While the surveys cover a range of sectors, we focus on manufacturing and on formal firms only, generally those with five or more employees, to ensure strict comparability. Our analysis draws on studies already completed and also uses new measurements, including dimensions of ethnicity and ownership, when a more precise formulation of the relevant questions in recent surveys enables a more focused analysis for a number of the countries. Finally, although we do present country-level data in various sections of the book, our analysis focuses more on *intra-country* variation in performance than on inter-country differences.

The total sample includes some 5,000 observations from the following countries: Angola, Benin, Botswana, Burkina Faso, Burundi, Cameroon, Cape Verde, the Democratic Republic of Congo, the Gambia, Guinea-Bissau, Guinea, Kenya, Lesotho, Madagascar, Malawi, Mali, Mauritania, Mauritius, Mozambique, Namibia, Niger, Rwanda, Senegal, South Africa, Swaziland, Tanzania, Uganda, and Zambia. Appropriate statistical tests were applied to determine the adequacy of the sample size relative to the population; particularly in small African economies, the population of formal firms can be small enough, relative to the surveys, to require use of sampling statistics without replacement.[3] Figure 1-2 shows the size distribution of firms in the data. Small firms are defined as having between five and fifty employees, medium firms as having between fifty-one and ninety-nine, and large firms as having 100 or more.

The analysis below has a number of limitations. It does not cover agriculture or other natural resource sectors, such as mining and forestry, although agribusiness, food processing, and wood processing are included. Neither does it cover informal firms or those with less than five employees. It also does not take as core countries middle-income countries such as South Africa, Botswana, or Mauritius, although survey results from these countries

2. Data are collected at the establishment level for each plant or operation rather than for the company as a whole. For a company with operations in multiple locations, each location is treated as a separate observation.

3. Full details of the sampling strategy for the Enterprise Surveys, along with the methodology for replacement sampling, is available at www.enterprisesurveys.org.

Figure 1-2. Size Distribution of Firms in the Sample

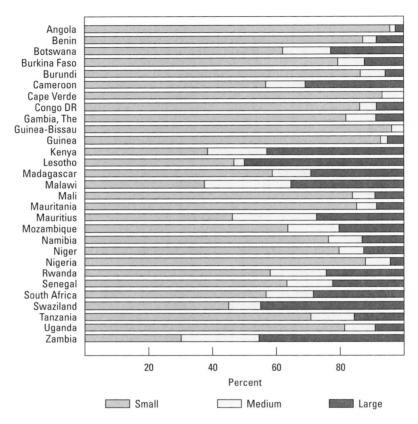

Source: World Bank Enterprise Surveys (www.enterprisesurveys.org).

are noted where relevant. As pointed out above, formal manufacturing is not a high share of GDP in most low-income African countries. Yet it is a critical sector, and it is one that experiences most of the constraints that all firms in the African private sector face. While manufacturing may not be the natural path for all countries, the investment climate constraints identified by firms in this sector will be largely the same for firms in other sectors. Also, many countries will need to move into manufacturing—including resource processing—as they transition out of agriculture in order to supply the domestic market, markets in neighboring countries, or international markets.

Camels versus Hippos

Do the data reflect the complete picture? Or are they badly contaminated by self-selection—do they miss the real story because they do not consider information from firms that have chosen *not* to locate in Africa or from firms that simply do not exist? That question is raised in Hausmann and Velasco (2005) in an anecdote about camels and hippos. If you interviewed some camels about living and working in a desert, you would get a very different idea of the main problems involved (perhaps heavy loads and mean camel drivers) than you would if you interviewed some hippos, which live in rivers, lakes, and wetlands. That implies that the really interesting thing to look at is the underlying industrial structure (the camel-to-hippo ratio in the desert), from which you can infer what other major problems might exist (for hippos and humans, no water).[4]

It is certainly true that the mix of firms surveyed will reflect a degree of self-selection, whether because of regulatory and governance issues or other country characteristics. One would not expect to find many high-tech computer firms in Burundi or a vibrant shipbuilding industry in Botswana.[5] Further, as discussed below, there are indications in the survey results that severe infrastructure constraints in some countries force firms to self-limit their operations and markets. However, there also are several indications that suggest that in practice, sorting effects do not dominate the firms' responses.

First, within countries, responses are relatively uniform across types of firm, including foreign-owned firms, whose managers presumably are better able to compare the quality of business environments across countries. In fact, major deviations in responses across types of firm occur only where expected (for example, foreign firms are less constrained and small firms are more constrained by finance).

Second, across countries, the intensity of complaints often correlates with macro-level country indicators. For example, complaints about finance are far more prevalent in countries with low financial depth. Using the camels-

---

4. We are grateful to George Clarke for discussions on this subject.

5. The approach taken by the World Economic Forum to construct its annual competitiveness report adjusts for country differences by weighting different constraints differently at different levels of development. The proposition that firms self-select is also implicit in theories of comparative advantage, which can be shaped by costs of non-traded goods and services as well as factor proportions. In extreme cases, the economy will consist of only subsistence farming and offshore oil rigs or, as in rural Niger, cattle farming.

and-hippos argument, firms in countries with low financial depth should be self-selected and not see low financial depth as an especially severe constraint.

Third, perhaps the most convincing evidence is generated by looking at firms that have actually adjusted to a constraint. Firms are not passive in the face of constraints. When possible they will adjust to them, giving rise to the question of whether the ability to adjust (presumably at some cost) means that the constraint is no longer considered serious. To answer that question, we ask another—whether perceptions about the electric power constraint are affected by ownership of a generator (figure 1-3). The results show that firms do not identify absent or unreliable power as less constraining when they own a generator. Firms with generators actually complain slightly more about electricity in many countries, perhaps because they tend to be more dependent on electricity and because generator power costs about three times more than power from the grid.

Evidence that generator ownership has no impact on a firm's perception of lack of power as a severe constraint suggests that firms recognize a constraint even when they can adapt to it. It suggests, for example, that firms that are able to secure services by paying large and costly bribes will nevertheless recognize the need to pay bribes as a constraint. Indeed, the camels-and-hippos argument can be turned around. If the self-selection process for firms is incomplete (as suggested above), the constraints identified by those present will likely be seen as *even more serious* by those firms that have *not* chosen to enter. If even camels would like to have more water in the desert (as we suspect that they generally would), the data suggest that a host of other animals would come in if the water constraint was alleviated. Alleviating Uganda's severe power constraint, for example, could bring in a multitude of new firms as well as improve conditions for established firms.

Another important issue to consider up front is whether much of the private sector's performance can simply be attributed to overvaluation of exchange rates in Africa. African countries do tend to have higher price levels than those predicted by the Balassa-Samuelson rule, which holds that lower relative price levels for non-tradables in poorer countries translate into lower overall price levels. Earlier rounds of purchasing power parity (PPP) data, admittedly rough, indicated that prices in Africa's low-income countries were higher in absolute terms than prices in China and South Asia and about 30 percent above the level predicted by per capita income; in comparison, prices in Asia were 13 to 20 percent below predictions (Eifert, Gelb, and Ramachandran 2008). Our analysis confirms the tendency for African prices to be higher than expected and for Asian prices to be lower.

Figure 1-3. Firms Ranking the Electricity Constraint as Major or Severe, Disaggregated by Generator Ownership

Percent

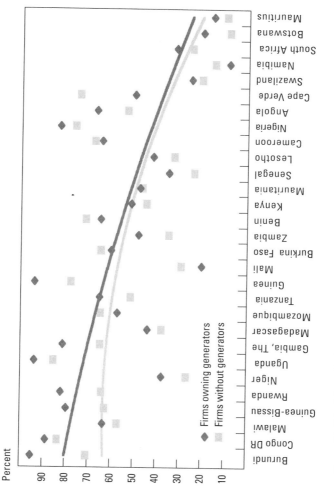

Source: World Bank Enterprise Surveys (www.enterprisesurveys.org).

High costs may also be associated with export structure. Eifert, Gelb, and Ramachandran (2008) considered forty-two low-income countries and found that price levels in those countries, where manufactures comprised a major share of exports, were typically below those predicted by the Balassa curve, while price levels in countries exporting fewer manufactured goods were above predicted levels. Repeating this analysis with new PPP data released at the end of 2007, we again find that to be the case: many countries in Africa are above the trend line in terms of their price levels relative to their levels of income. More recently, Johnson, Ostry, and Subramanian (2007), which found a similar result, argues that overvaluation of the exchange rate is problematic in several African countries.

While prices are indeed high, we do not believe that exchange rate misalignment is the main explanation. It is not unreasonable to think that African exchange rates continue to be modestly overvalued because of large-scale aid flows and resulting Dutch disease effects. It may be that overvaluation raises the prices of inputs by about 20 percent or so. But when African firms were asked about the prices that they paid for raw materials, the responses that they provided indicate that prices were *two to three times* what firms in China paid (Eifert, Gelb, and Ramachandran 2008). That cannot be due entirely to exchange rate overvaluation.

The data do show that in Africa, the price of capital goods is very high relative to the price of consumption goods. But they also show that there is a fair bit of variation across sectors and firms. Exchange rate overvaluation cannot generate price imbalances within countries between different sectors—the imbalances must be driven by other factors.

Finally, exchange rate overvaluation should affect the cost of domestic inputs relative to imported inputs rather than the total cost of inputs. That is, it should be relatively cheap for African firms to import capital and inputs from abroad and relatively expensive to use domestic inputs. For example, aid-related Dutch disease makes it difficult for a country to compete in tradable goods by lowering the relative price of imports and raising the relative price of exports. But we observe very high costs for imported inputs (including capital) and often low quality as well—neither of which seems to be explained very well by exchange rate overvaluation.

two

The Business Environment in Sub-Saharan Africa

We have had no significant capital injection into generation and transmission, from either the private or public sectors, for fifteen, maybe twenty years.

LAWRENCE MUSABA, *Southern Africa Power Pool*[1]

How do firms see their business environment in Africa, and how does business climate affect productivity? The data presented in this chapter summarize key aspects of the business environment and the kinds of burdens that firms face in their day-to-day operations. As shown below, there are many similarities in the business environments across low-income countries in Africa. We begin by looking at firms' subjective perceptions of their operating environment and then move on to more objective measures of the business environment.

What Matters Most to African Businesses?

What factors are most constraining to firms in Africa? Do the worst constraints vary systematically by country or by groups of countries? One way to answer those questions is to ask the firms themselves. Ratings of the severity

1. Quoted in Wines (2007).

19

of constraints are provided by businesses' *perceptions* of constraints, as documented separately from the objective indicators in the Enterprise Survey data. The surveys identify seventeen common constraints. Each constraint is considered to be a perceived impediment if a firm rates it as "major" or "severe." The percentage of firms rating constraints in either of the two categories is considered to be the indicator of severity for a country.

Are these ratings really rankings? Experience suggests that they are a mix. Faced with an especially serious constraint, firms are less likely to emphasize other constraints, even if the latter are serious; to some degree the ranking will affect ratings. On the other hand, firms in countries that have a business climate that is relatively good are also less likely to rate obstacles as major or severe, suggesting that the responses are not simply rankings.

Figures 2-1, 2-2, and 2-3 illustrate the responses for constraints of several types across countries, ordered in terms of rising level of income per capita. In the least developed countries in our sample—Burundi, the Democratic Republic of Congo, Malawi, Guinea-Bissau, Rwanda, Niger, Uganda, the Gambia, and Madagascar—manufacturing firms are most likely to be concerned about the most fundamental constraints to doing business. Is there a reliable power supply? Can financing be secured? Is it possible to obtain serviced land? Can the firm plan ahead, or does macroeconomic instability make that impossible?

In some of these countries, individual constraints can be serious enough to be considered truly binding. For example, electricity tariffs in Uganda would have to increase to almost US$0.29 per kilowatt hour (kWh) if the consumer were to bear the full cost of electricity, including the expensive thermal generation used in attempts to plug capacity gaps. The cost of load shedding to the economy is significant, and expensive back-up generation has affected the competitiveness of industrial production. The cost of additional energy to address unmet demand has been estimated at about US$0.39 per kWh, excluding multiplier effects (Power Planning Associates 2007). Not surprisingly, 87 percent of Ugandan firms considered electricity a major or severe constraint in 2006. Even in South Africa, which has long enjoyed a power surplus, things started to change dramatically toward the end of the survey period, as several cities began to experience rolling blackouts. The losses associated with power outages, as estimated by the firms, can amount to more than 10 percent of sales in some countries. As discussed later, such losses tend to be reflected in a similar loss in overall productivity.

Access to finance remains problematic even after the power situation improves, and other constraints do not die away completely as the business environment improves. In South Africa, for example, macroeconomic instability is rated a serious problem by many exporters concerned about the volatility of the rand.

A second set of problems tends to become more serious than basic business constraints as countries move up the ladder toward lower-middle-income status. In countries such as Tanzania, Guinea, Mali, Burkina Faso, Zambia, Benin, Kenya, Mauritania, Senegal, Lesotho, and Cameroon, weak governance and low administrative and bureaucratic capacity are serious concerns, evident in the tax system (rates and especially tax administration), in government corruption, and in the control of crime and violence, which, as shown below, imposes high costs on many firms. Poor governance, of course, may also be responsible for some of the elemental constraints (for example, corruption can mean that investments in power generation do not go ahead or are not effectual), but firms may not experience the effects of poor governance directly. Some aspects of regulation will be less troubling to firms in environments in which governance is weak. Even if labor laws are stringent, the weak capacity of the state to enforce them means that they are less likely to be perceived as a serious problem, certainly relative to other factors.

A third set of factors tends to be most problematic for firms in the more developed, highest-income group, including Cape Verde, Swaziland, Namibia, South Africa, Botswana, and Mauritius. Figure 2-3 sketches their perceptions of labor policies and shortages of skilled labor. It is notable that in most countries, even those that are more sophisticated and have higher incomes, concern about the latter exceeds concern about the former. Why might labor regulation be seen as a more serious problem at higher levels of development? Unless higher income is due to exogenous factors such as large hydrocarbon deposits, institutions tend to become stronger and the state tends to become more capable at higher levels of income. Concerns about infrastructure, access to finance, corruption, and access to land decrease considerably; even concerns about crime fall relative to perceived difficulties in the low-middle-income category. But business is not the only constituency in such countries—labor also exercises its voice, and regulations need to balance the interests of employers and employees.[2]

These data on firms' perceptions suggest at least three areas for us to investigate in greater detail—infrastructure, governance and the regulatory

---

2. Given that the emphasis of this book is on low-income Africa, we do not focus on labor policy here, but we do explore these results in other work (Gelb and others 2007).

Figure 2-1. Firms Ranking an Elemental Constraint as Major or Severe, ordered by GDP per Capita[a]

Percent

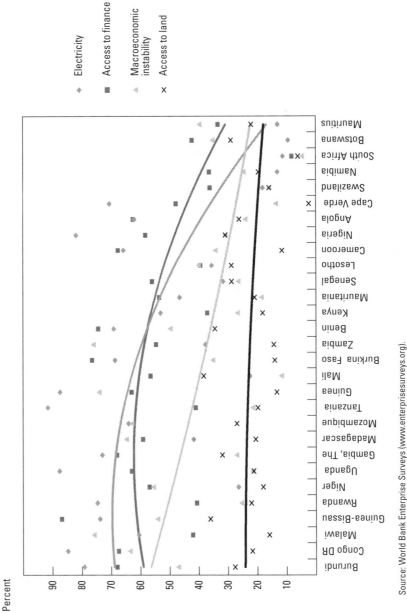

Legend:
- ◆ Electricity
- ■ Access to finance
- ◀ Macroeconomic instability
- ✕ Access to land

Source: World Bank Enterprise Surveys (www.enterprisesurveys.org).
a. The relative importance of elemental constraints tends to decline as income increases.

Figure 2-2. Firms Ranking a Governance Constraint as Major or Severe, ordered by GDP per Capita[a]

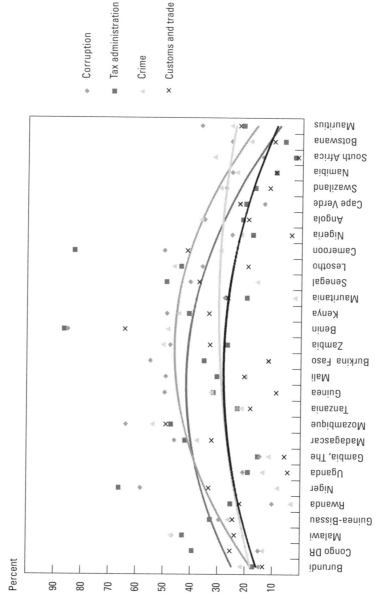

Percent

- ◆ Corruption
- ■ Tax administration
- ◀ Crime
- ✕ Customs and trade

Source: World Bank Enterprise Surveys (www.enterprisesurveys.org).
a. Governance constraints tend to peak in the middle of the income range.

Figure 2-3. Firms Ranking a Labor Constraint as Major or Severe, ordered by GDP per Capita[a]

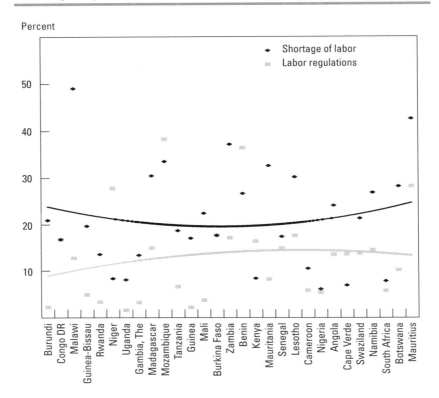

Source: World Bank Enterprise Surveys (www.enterprisesurveys.org).
a. Concerns about labor policy and worker skills tend to peak at the high end of the income range.

environment, and access to finance. We focus our analysis in these areas, using more objective measures provided by the Enterprise Surveys, to complement the data on perceptions described above. In the area of access to finance, we consider the situation of smaller, black-owned firms specifically. That is not to say that other areas of the business environment are not important for specific countries or even for the region as a whole. Our approach here is to look at what emerges as a key constraint from the point of view of the business sector to try to understand why the manufacturing sector in Africa is growing so slowly.

Infrastructure: Power and Transport

There is perhaps no greater burden on African firms than the lack of a reliable supply of electric power. Figure 2-4 shows the number of days on which a power outage was reported across countries. A handful of countries— Namibia, South Africa, Mauritius, and Botswana—reported outages on fewer than ten days in the year. Firms in six countries—Mali, Lesotho, Swaziland, Senegal, Guinea-Bissau, and Zambia—reported outages on between ten and fifty days. Firms located in the remaining countries experienced outages on more than fifty days in the year. The worst cases were the Gambia, Guinea, and the Democratic Republic of Congo (each with more than 150 days of outages); Uganda, Rwanda, and Tanzania were not far behind. It is fair to say that an outage occurs almost every working day in these countries, excluding weekends and holidays. It is worth noting that power outages are not just frequent but also lengthy. The average length of an outage in Africa is five hours; in some countries, the average length is more than twelve hours.

How do firms cope? Not very well and at high cost. In Cameroon, Rwanda, Guinea, Senegal, the Gambia, Angola, Guinea-Bissau, and Kenya, more than 50 percent of firms own generators to offset the load shedding and erratic supply provided by the public grid. Even in very low-income countries such as Madagascar, Niger, Benin, and Mauritania, about 20 to 30 percent of firms own generators. Kenya, where 70 percent of firms own generators, tops the list; electricity is now an even greater constraint than corruption, about which Kenyan firms have long complained. The ability of enterprises to offset power fluctuations varies greatly by enterprise size. Figure 2-5 shows that for the most part, only larger firms (those with 100 or more employees) are able to cope with Africa's power crisis. In Zambia, for example, large enterprises are twenty times more likely to own a generator than small and medium-size enterprises (SMEs). In Mauritania, 100 percent of large firms own generators, as they do in Niger, the Gambia, and Cape Verde. That figure is anywhere from two and a half to five times the rate of generator ownership among SMEs in these countries.

Perhaps no country in Africa suffers more from power outages than Nigeria. Data from surveys and other sources show that almost 40 percent of electricity is privately provided through generators. In 2005, researchers in Nigeria found that the cost of electricity from generators was three times the cost of electricity from the public grid—5 versus 15 naira per kWh (Adenikinju 2005). Almost all firms owned generators, of varying quality and vintage,

Figure 2-4. Number of Days on which Power Outages Occurred

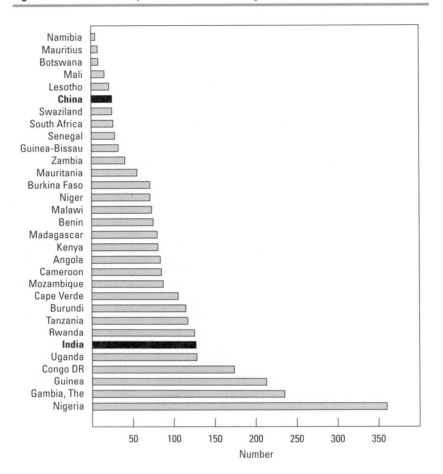

Source: World Bank Enterprise Surveys (www.enterprisesurveys.org).

in an attempt to offset the load shedding and erratic supply provided by the Nigerian Electric Power Authority (NEPA—often referred to by the citizenry as "No Electricity Presently Available"). Fuel is sometimes hard to find in this oil-exporting country, and maintenance of generator equipment imposes further costs on firms (World Bank 2001).

Frequent outages impose a substantial loss in terms of sales (figure 2-6). For those countries in which a question about the impact of outages was

Figure 2-5. Firms Owning Generators

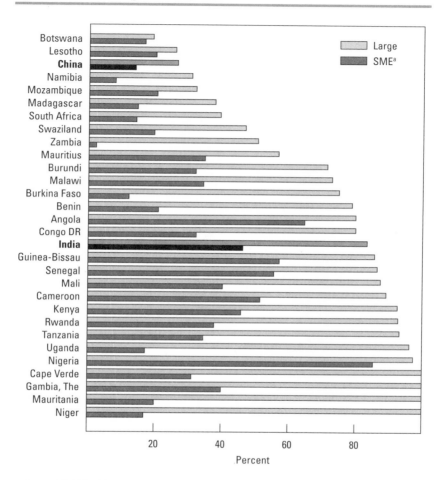

Source: World Bank Enterprise Surveys (www.enterprisesurveys.org).
a. SME = small and medium-size enterprises (less than 100 workers).

asked, losses were estimated to be up to one-third of the wage bill. Moreover, the percentage of sales losses is mirrored in productivity losses. Energy as a share of total costs also is high for African firms (figure 2-7). Firms in Mozambique, Benin, Burkina Faso, Senegal, the Gambia, Madagascar, and Niger spend more than 10 percent of their total costs on energy. In China, the cost of energy is only 3 percent of total costs. As mentioned previously, much of

Figure 2-6. Estimated Sales Lost Due to Power Outages

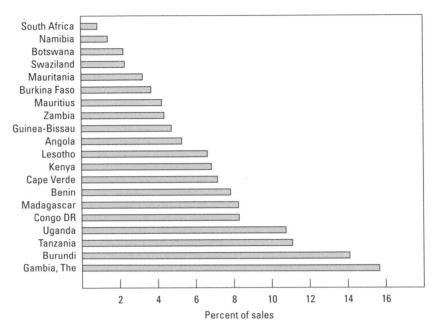

Source: World Bank Enterprise Surveys (www.enterprisesurveys.org).

South Africa currently experiences rolling blackouts. Additional data on the cost of energy for selected countries (not reported here) show that the median number of hours of each outage is anywhere from two hours a day to almost nineteen hours a day across the continent!

Given such data, it is not surprising that the responses of businesses to the question regarding their *most* severe constraint overwhelmingly indicate that lack of a reliable supply of electrical power is the key constraint in much of sub-Saharan Africa. Almost half of all businesses surveyed indicated that it was their worst problem. In late July 2007, twenty-five of the forty-four countries in sub-Saharan Africa were experiencing crippling power shortages (Wines 2007). Currently, several major cities experience daily blackouts. More recently, power outages of several hours a day led opposition parties in South Africa to call for the termination of power supply arrangements with other countries, and outraged commuters in Pretoria set fire to trains in early

Figure 2-7. Energy as a Share of Total Cost

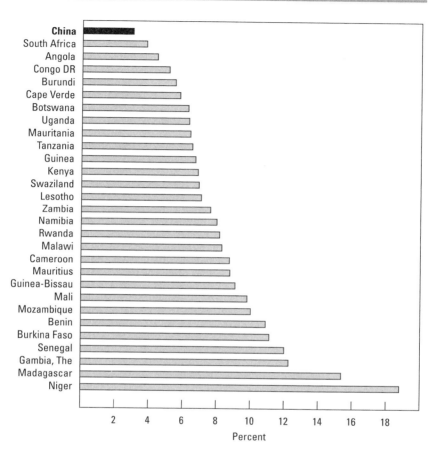

Source: World Bank Enterprise Surveys (www.enterprisesurveys.org).

January 2008 when the power went out for several hours and shut down parts of the transit system (Shaw 2008).

Transport is almost as serious a problem as power. The limited availability and high cost of physical infrastructure in sub-Saharan Africa—including roads, railways, and air transport—also put a brake on private sector competitiveness. The low-income economies of sub-Saharan Africa lag far behind those in developing countries in other parts of the world in terms of paved roads and modern freight and passenger transport systems. The lack of adequate transportation has a direct impact on the level of business activity because it lowers productivity and limits the entry of new firms. Poor transport affects firms in two ways—poor-quality roads cause loss of goods and trading opportunities, while delays and losses in transit, including those due to roadblocks, relate to poor governance. Firms in Africa either supply only fragmented regional markets or restrict themselves to market opportunities in which profits are high enough to cover high transport costs.

Transport bottlenecks typically are a long-term problem, unlike the power supply, which can improve or deteriorate rapidly. Bad roads and limited transnational links usually are well known to the private sector, and they lead to self-selection of markets and activities. This geographical sparseness of economic activity, as described in the previous chapter, means that production technologies are likely to be exogenously transport-intensive.

Keeping these problems in mind, we look at the ranking of transport bottlenecks by firms that are in the market. In the Enterprise Surveys, firms were asked whether transport problems present an obstacle to firm operation and growth, and the rankings show large differences across countries that are correlated with overall level of economic development and infrastructure. In middle-income countries such as Botswana, South Africa, Mauritius, Swaziland, and Namibia, less that 20 percent of firms complain about transport problems, whereas in Kenya, 53 percent of firms consider transport to be a major obstacle. In very-low-income countries in Africa, the camels-hippo effect comes in—the vast majority of firms sell their goods only in the local market and do not even consider selling their goods anywhere else. Survey results therefore *underestimate* the problem of transport bottlenecks.

Figure 2-8 shows that transport also is a very real constraint for larger businesses (those of 100 or more employees). In most countries large firms are more likely to complain about transport than smaller businesses. They account for a large share of manufacturing employment and industrial value added, and they are most likely to expand beyond local markets. Yet, in a region with few navigable waterways, in all but the richest countries in our sample, less than half of inputs were delivered by road. Many firms rely on costly air shipments to meet their needs. A manager of a large cement manufacturing company commented that he occasionally airlifts cement across countries—probably an unheard of method of delivery in any other part of the world.

Finally, firms were asked about losses due to transport failures—the percentage of consignment value lost due to theft or breakage in transit. These

Figure 2-8. Businesses Ranking Transport as a Major or Severe Obstacle, Disaggregated by Size

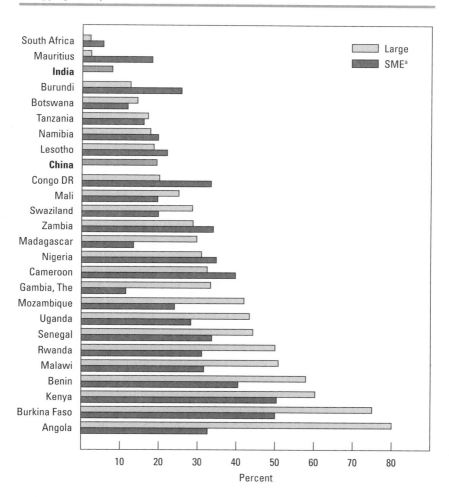

Source: World Bank Enterprise Surveys (www.enterprisesurveys.org).
a. SME = small and medium-size enterprises (less than 100 workers).

losses are presented in figure 2-9. Firms in the low-income economies of sub-Saharan Africa suffer the most, and larger firms suffer greater losses than smaller ones. The losses incurred are much higher than those in China or India, where the average loss for large firms is just 1.3 percent of consignment value. Of course, lack of roads and power does not affect just manufacturing

Figure 2-9. Estimated Losses from Breakage, Theft, and Delays in Transport

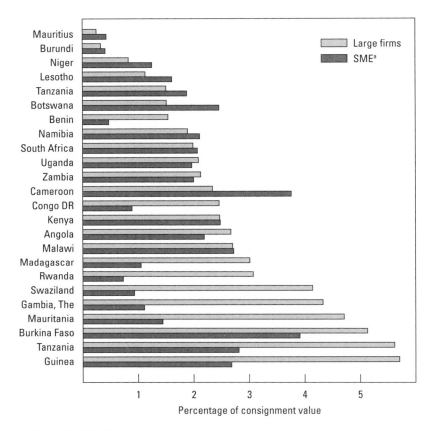

Percentage of consignment value

Source: World Bank Enterprise Surveys (www.enterprisesurveys.org).
a. SME = small and medium-size enterprises (less than 100 workers).

but agriculture as well—the lack of infrastructure has meant that farmers often are unable to increase value added through processing or to transport their goods overland to domestic markets or international ports.

The Regulatory Environment

The regulatory burden on African firms has been the focus of much attention in recent years, due at least in part to the World Bank's *Doing Business* reports. According to *Doing Business* data, African firms suffer some of the most bur-

Table 2-1. Days to Get Utility Connections and Permits

Country	Telephone	Electricity	Water	Construction permit	Import license
Angola	265.1	79.1	81.3	50.8	20.5
Benin	159.7	70.4	62.0	125.3	38.2
Botswana	25.8	32.7	14.1	79.5	26.5
Burkina Faso	44.8	22.3	24.0	45.0	2.1
Burundi	34.6	51.8	30.0	152.3	6.6
Cameroon	73.1	62.9	84.2	109.4	17.2
Congo DR	16.9	47.6	21.9	29.0	11.7
Gambia, The	15.8	76.5	11.1	47.7	7.4
Guinea	115.4	30.9	22.2	36.3	13.9
Guinea-Bissau	25.9	25.6	80.0	38.1	27.5
Kenya	34.2	52.1	25.9	34.0	13.4
Lesotho	101.8	43.3	57.3	141.1	7.3
Madagascar	60.4	47.3	n/a	n/a	17.9
Malawi	100.7	100.5	71.6	72.6	26.2
Mali	70.6	35.3	32.4	69.0	32.7
Mauritania	12.0	20.9	27.8	22.2	1.6
Mauritius	25.3	22.3	27.5	113.0	8.5
Mozambique	29.2	n/a	n/a	n/a	n/a
Namibia	8.5	13.2	18.8	11.5	8.4
Niger	24.7	40.6	116.8	4.8	13.1
Nigeria	8.3	8.2	12.5	12.8	25.4
Rwanda	n/a	n/a	25.4	5.0	6.1
South Africa	6.5	4.6	8.3	8.0	5.9
Senegal	17.0	13.2	9.4	57.4	18.2
Swaziland	20.5	11.7	n/a	29.9	9.2
Tanzania	22.6	52.8	28.0	47.9	16.8
Uganda	15.1	41.4	22.7	15.6	18.9
Zambia	88.5	184.1	26.8	34.3	11.4
China	6.8	18.5	n/a	n/a	n/a
India	12.0	26.1	17.7	n/a	n/a

Source: World Bank Enterprise Surveys (www.enterprisesurveys.org).

densome regulations in the world. In the "ease of doing business" rankings of 178 countries provided in these reports, only two African countries (Mauritius and South Africa) are in the top fifty; another two countries—Kenya and Ghana—are in the top 100. The remaining countries are mostly at the bottom (World Bank 2001–07). Despite various reform efforts and decades of technical assistance, government responsiveness and delivery of basic services remain problematic in many countries. Regulatory weaknesses exacerbate the problems caused by a lack of physical infrastructure.

The number of days to get other utility connections is shown in table 2-1. Obtaining water, telephone, and electric services is not easy—apart from a handful of countries, firms in much of Africa must wait several days and

Table 2-2. Trade Indicators

Country	Cost to export (US$ per container)	Cost to import (US$ per container)	Trade integration (trade as percent of GDP)
Angola	1850	2325	97.2
Benin	1167	1202	48.1
Botswana	2328	2595	87.6
Burkina Faso	2096	3522	32.5
Burundi	2147	3705	63.6
Cameroon	907	1529	50.3
Cape Verde	1024	1024	110.2
Congo, Dem. Rep.	2307	2183	92.8
Congo, Rep.	2201	2201	122.6
Eritrea	1331	1581	56.4
Ethiopia	1617	2793	50.0
Gabon	1510	1600	94.2
Gambia, The	809	869	95.1
Ghana	895	895	105.5
Guinea	570	995	75.6
Guinea-Bissau	1445	1749	80.9
Kenya	1955	1995	55.9
Lesotho	1188	1210	158.1
Madagascar	1182	1282	66.3
Malawi	1623	2500	70.8
Mali	1752	2680	66.6
Mauritania	1360	1363	125.4
Mauritius	728	673	131.1
Mozambique	1155	1185	95.7
Namibia	1539	1550	102.4
Niger	2945	2946	46.8
Nigeria	1026	1047	76.4
Rwanda	2975	4970	39.2
Senegal	828	1720	77.9
South Africa	1087	1195	67.1
Tanzania	1212	1425	60.8
Uganda	2940	2990	47.1
Zambia	2098	2840	74.6
China	390	430	75.6
India	820	910	45.2
Indonesia	623	667	56.7
United States	1160	960	28.6

Source: World Trade Indicators 2008 (www.worldbank.org/wti2008).

sometimes months to get connections. Construction permits and import licenses also are fairly hard to come by. China does very well in comparison with almost every African country in the table.

Table 2-2 and figure 2-10 show that the cost in terms of money and time of importing and exporting goods in Africa is high compared with costs in India and China. The cost of exporting or importing a container of goods is

Figure 2-10. Days to Comply with Trade-Related Regulations

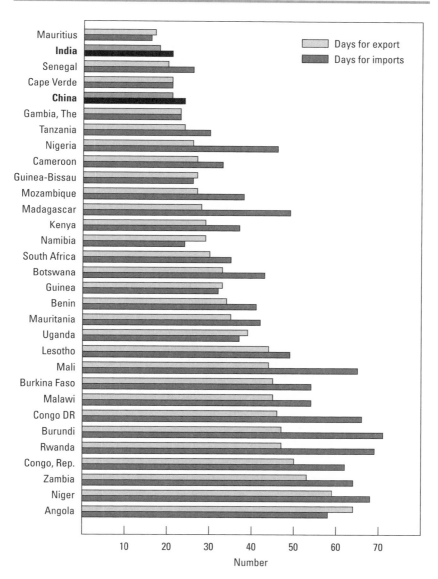

Source: World Bank (2001–07).

as much as four or five times the cost in China and two or three times that in India. In much of sub-Saharan Africa, it takes weeks to comply with trade-related regulations in order to ship goods in and out of ports. If the goods being exported are perishable or are otherwise of a time-sensitive nature, such shipping times are a great burden to export businesses; a useful rule of thumb is that for time-sensitive products, a one-day delay is equivalent to a 1 percent drop in sales price. That does not compare well with shipping times in China, where it takes only a few days to comply with regulations to turn goods around at port and the process is nowhere near as expensive as it is in Africa. India's times are good but financial costs are high; however, it is worth remembering that India has a far larger economy and its share of trade in GDP is far lower than the share in many countries in Africa.

The survey data also show that managers spend between 5 and 10 percent of their time dealing with regulators. However, in about nine countries, managers spend well over that amount of time; in Lesotho and Madagascar, for example, managers spend almost 20 percent of their time dealing with the government.

Firms in most African countries also need to pay bribes to get things done, whether to obtain a utility connection, a license, or an evaluation from an inspector that allows the firm to continue operations (figure 2-11). Due to the sensitive nature of the questions and the fact that firms often fear retaliation, they were not asked whether they paid bribes but rather whether bribes "are necessary in their industry." The responses were used to infer what percentage of firms paid bribes. Data from a small number of countries in our sample—South Africa, Cape Verde, Namibia, Mauritius, Rwanda, Botswana, and Senegal—show that not more than 20 percent of firms paid bribes. With the exception of Rwanda, they are some of the higher-income countries in our sample. Between 20 and 50 percent of firms in a large group of countries indicated that bribes were necessary. In our final group—Mali, Kenya, Mauritania, Democratic Republic of Congo, and Guinea-Bissau—the vast majority of firms appear to pay bribes. The percentage of sales estimated to be lost in paying bribes also varies across countries—from much less than 1 percent in the higher-income countries to well over 3 percent in several other countries in our sample. It is useful to think about bribes as an additional burden to firms, besides the high cost of energy, other indirect costs, and energy-related and transport losses.

Since 2001, the World Bank's *Doing Business* database has provided information on the cost of setting up a business. The data are not based on surveys but on the costs faced by a "median firm" operating under the laws of the country in which it is located. Table 2-3 summarizes the cost and the days

Figure 2-11. Firms Paying Bribes

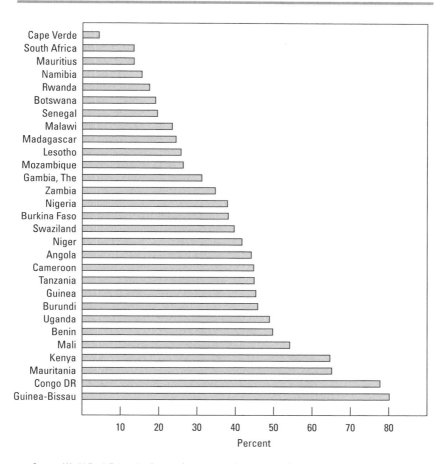

Source: World Bank Enterprise Surveys (www.enterprisesurveys.org).

required to register a firm in the twenty-seven African countries included in this analysis and gives the global ranking of each. The *Doing Business* data show that the cost of starting a business is generally very high. Of the 178 countries ranked in the ease of doing business index, only one African country (Mauritius) is in the top fifty and only a few more are in the top 100. Most African countries are ranked at or near the bottom of the list. While India does not do a whole lot better, China is ranked more highly than almost all the African countries on the list.

Table 2-3. The Time and Cost of Starting a Business

Country	Ease of doing business rank	Rank	Procedures (number)	Time (days)	Cost (percentage of income per capita)	Minimum capital (percentage of income per capita)
Angola	167	173	12	119	343.7	50.5
Benin	151	137	7	31	195	354.2
Botswana	51	99	11	108	9.9	0
Burkina Faso	161	105	6	18	82.1	415.7
Burundi	174	124	11	43	251	0
Cameroon	154	160	13	37	129.2	177.1
Cape Verde	132	156	12	52	40.1	53.4
Congo DR	178	146	13	155	487.2	0
Gambia, The	131	94	9	32	279	0
Guinea	166	171	13	41	138.3	466.5
Guinea-Bissau	176	178	17	233	255.5	1,006.6
Kenya	72	112	12	44	46.1	0
Lesotho	124	126	8	73	37.4	14.3
Madagascar	149	61	5	7	22.7	333.4
Malawi	127	108	10	37	188.7	0
Mali	158	149	11	26	132.1	434.6
Mauritania	157	167	11	65	56.2	503.1
Mauritius	27	8	6	7	5.3	0
Mozambique	134	125	10	29	21.6	115.8
Namibia	43	101	10	99	22.3	0
Niger	169	153	11	23	174.8	735.6
Rwanda	150	63	9	16	171.5	0
Senegal	162	159	10	58	107	255
South Africa	35	53	8	31	7.1	0
Swaziland	95	142	13	61	38.7	0.6
Tanzania	130	95	12	29	47.1	0
Uganda	118	114	18	28	92	0
Zambia	116	82	6	33	30.5	2.2
China	83	135	13	35	8.4	190.2
India	120	111	13	33	74.6	0

Source: World Bank (2001–07).

What are some of the factors underlying those numbers? It may well be that weak governance has led to firms that are exogenously intensive in their use of bribes, informal payments, and private security costs. In an analysis of the political economy of reform, Emery (2003) notes that the "overall complexity [of doing business] places a premium on means of circumventing, or speeding up the process, which creates a flourishing environment for corruption." Emery argues that most firms in Africa are operating outside the law in at least one or more respects and are vulnerable to government inspectors, no matter how minor the deviance. The survival of a business is consequently heavily dependent on a personal relationship with a minister or other high government official that often is difficult to document or quantify. Such relationships are crucial to firms that need to anticipate ad hoc policy or regulatory changes. Emery concludes that "this vulnerability, combined with the arbitrary nature of enforcement arising from poor governance means that firms can be closed down or worse for operating in exactly the same way as their neighbors, their competitors, or their clients and suppliers."

Dismantling some of the key controls that governments continue to maintain is consequently difficult. Sources of both patronage and control can be used to penalize firms that represent a political threat. While the situation is changing, sometimes quite quickly, some governments still seem to fear a private sector that generates wealth independent of government control and makes its own, unfettered decisions. Reforms that target individual regulations are therefore less likely to succeed over the long term.

Finally, a word on how Africa's business environment compares with that of China and India. From the data presented above, it can be seen that the business environments in these two manufacturing giants are well ahead of Africa's in many respects. In many areas, China's business environment also appears to be better than that of India and well ahead of that in almost every African country, including the middle-income countries in the sample. The differences between Africa and India are less clear. Some aspects of India's regulatory costs and electricity problems seem to be comparable with Africa's, but it is useful to remember that India also lags China quite substantially in the manufacturing sector. Research by Lall and Mengistae shows that a significant part of India's productivity lag can be explained by the severity of its power shortages (Lall and Mengistae 2005a and 2005b). But certain costs are less critical for a large economy like India, especially those related to trade, and in a number of important areas, including security, it rates substantially better than Africa.

So why does Africa lag behind? To address that question, we turn to an analysis of business performance and market structure, which is followed by a discussion of political economy factors that determine the supply of entrepreneurs. While high costs themselves might not be a sufficient explanation for Africa's performance, the interaction of the high-cost business environment with political economy factors may help explain why growth has been so slow.

Is Access to Credit a Problem?

As noted, many African firms complain about lack of access to credit. There is a large literature that looks in depth at that issue in sub-Saharan Africa

(Ayyagari, Demirguc-Kunt, and Maksimovic 2006; Bigsten and others 2000; Raturi and Swamy 1999). The reasons for lack of access include the lack of depth in the formal banking sector (which limits access for all businesses), crowding out due to public sector debt (which also limits financial flows to the private sector), selective lending to establishments with connections to the banking authorities, and high collateral requirements and costs of capital that ration out all but the most profitable businesses. Others have argued that indigenous firms are at a special disadvantage—they are rationed out by the banking sector due to their lack of credit history. Supplier credit also is constrained for this group because of lack of information networks and reputation channels.[3] It is clear that firms rank access to finance as a very serious concern in many countries in Africa.

Figures 2-12 and 2-13 show the sources of finance used by firms in the entire sample, as well as the percentage whose accounts were audited. We see that most firms used internal sources of financing for their operations, which implies that access to finance might be problematic. But we also see that in many countries, a significant share of firms do not have their accounts audited, making it difficult for lenders to assess their creditworthiness.[4] Our data also show that small firms were far more likely to complain than larger firms. That raises the question of whether firms are truly credit constrained or whether it simply is not possible to assess their creditworthiness.

Learning Channels

Finally, a word on learning channels. In some surveys, firm owners are asked whether their firm has a website, whether it is ISO certified, and whether it offers a training program. We refer to these variables as "learning channels" because they likely represent means by which the firm can improve its productivity. Figure 2-14 shows that these variables generally are correlated with

---

3. The World Bank recently presented a comprehensive action plan for financial sector development in Africa in a report titled *Making Finance Work for Africa* (Honohan and Beck 2006). In it, the authors argued that the financial sector agenda needs to take a two-pronged approach—first, by focusing on the formal financial sector to improve access to finance for larger firms as well as for the housing and infrastructure sectors; second, by improving the access of low-income households and small entrepreneurs through microfinance and other mechanisms. Building on the momentum generated by the report, the G-8 summit in Heiligendamm, Germany, adopted the key message of the report in 2007.

4. The data for China and India, while not strictly comparable, reveal that firms in these countries do not use bank financing very much either. Only 20 percent of surveyed Chinese firms reported having a bank loan; the number was 30 percent for Indian firms. Interestingly, Indian firms reported heavy reliance on internal sources of finance (50 percent said that they used this type of financing) while 50 percent of Chinese firms reported the use of informal sources of finance.

Figure 2-12. Sources of Finance

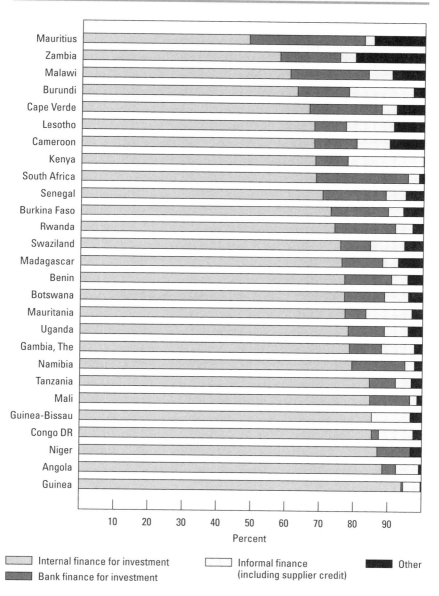

Source: World Bank Enterprise Surveys (www.enterprisesurveys.org).

Figure 2-13. Firms with Audited Accounts

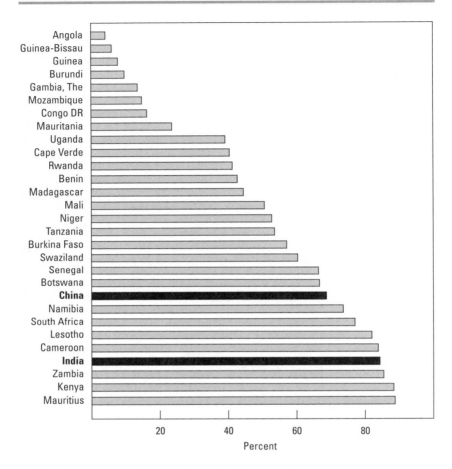

Source: World Bank Enterprise Surveys (www.enterprisesurveys.org).

income—firms in the richer countries in our survey were more likely to have a website or to be ISO certified.

The Performance of African Firms

How productive are African firms? How is their productivity affected by the adverse business environment? There is a considerable amount of research in this area that suggests that the productivity of firms in much of low-income

Figure 2-14. Share of Firms in Sample with Learning Channels

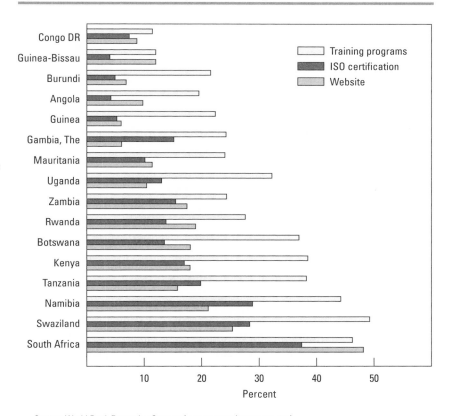

Source: World Bank Enterprise Surveys (www.enterprisesurveys.org).

Africa is low compared with that of firms elsewhere. The reasons given range from the lack of skilled labor to macroeconomic instability, exchange rate fluctuations, adverse business climate, and lack of institutional development (Guasch and Escribano 2005; Fafchamps 2004; Collier and Gunning 1997; Biggs, Srivastava, and Shah 1995; Soderbom and Teal 2003; Mazumdar and Mazaheri 2003; Dollar, Hallward-Driemeier, and Mengistae 2005).

Impact of the Business Environment

In earlier work we examined the impact on firm performance of high indirect costs rather than shortages, focusing on energy costs in particular. That analysis showed that the lack of good infrastructure and the overall fragility

Figure 2-15. Impact of the Business Environment: Average Gross versus Net Total Factor Value, Indexed Relative to China

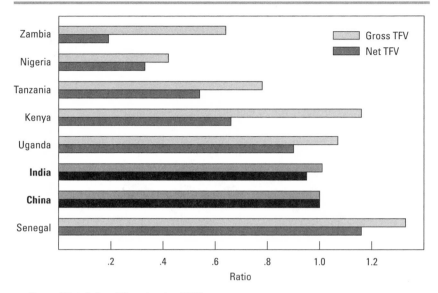

Source: Eifert, Gelb, and Ramachandran (2008).

of the business environment reduced the overall productivity of African firms vis-à-vis firms in other parts of the world (Eifert, Gelb, and Ramachandran 2008). The results are summarized in figure 2-15. "Gross" total factor value added is defined as sales minus the cost of raw materials, and "net" total factor value added is defined as sales minus the sum of raw materials and indirect costs—for example, for power, transport, licensing fees, and bribes. African firms look substantially less productive when indirect costs are accounted for—in some cases as much as 40 percent less productive.

The intuition behind this result is fairly straightforward. If a firm incurs very high costs due to the need to pay for security services and costly, unreliable power or to transport its goods long distances on poor-quality roads, those costs are not reflected in a standard performance metric generated from regressions of sales on labor, capital, and raw materials. But it will show up in augmented estimations, which include indirect costs as well. When they leave indirect inputs aside and focus exclusively on more traditional inputs of raw materials and capital, studies that attempt to benchmark the performance of manufacturing firms across countries in the developing

Figure 2-16. Impact of the Business Environment: Distribution of the Ratio of Net to Gross Value Added, Africa versus China, Kernel Density Estimation

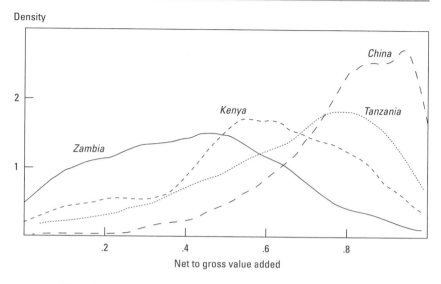

Source: Eifert, Gelb, and Ramachandran (2008).

world have typically underestimated the gap between African firms and their comparators elsewhere.

Figure 2-16 illustrates that effect. It shows the difference in the distributions of net and gross value added across firms within China, Kenya, Tanzania, and Zambia. The China distribution is heavily skewed to the right, with most of the mass of firms between 0.75–0.95. The African distributions have a great deal of mass on the left, in the 0.30–0.60 range, suggesting that many African firms see their ability to produce value beyond the cost of their direct and indirect inputs as heavily constrained by the magnitude of the cost of the latter. That is true in Zambia in particular, where the distribution is centered around 0.40.[5]

5. Several other studies have examined allocative efficiency and enterprise productivity using different approaches (Haltiwanger, Scarpetta, and Schweiger 2006; Escribano and Guasch 2005; Bastos and Nasir 2004; Biggs, Srivastava, and Shah 1995). Many of those studies show that an adverse business climate has a significant negative impact on firm performance. Other studies have found conflicting results, particularly when examining the role of regulation and governance in enterprise performance (Hallward-Driemeier, Wallsten, and Xu 2003). Reinikka and Svensson argue that a time tax on management due to a high regulatory burden can be positively correlated with productivity—firms that pay bribes are more productive than others (Reinikka and Svensson 2006).

Figure 2-17. Labor Productivity of Firms[a]

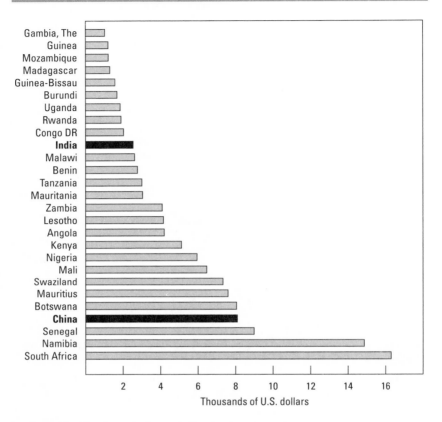

Thousands of U.S. dollars

Source: World Bank Enterprise Surveys (www.enterprisesurveys.org).
a. Labor productivity is measured as value added per worker in US$.

Labor Productivity

Figure 2-17 shows that enterprises in middle-income Africa have much higher labor productivity than those in low-income Africa. Average labor productivity in India is similar to that of lower-income African countries, while China's labor productivity is comparable to that of middle-income African countries. We also examined the entire distribution of the labor productivity of firms across different income groups in sub-Saharan Africa; those kernel density estimates are presented in figure 2-18. The figure shows that there is very little overlap in labor productivity between firms in middle-income and low-income African countries. The width of the distribution,

Figure 2-18. Distribution of Labor Productivity (Log), by Level of Income, Kernel Density Estimations

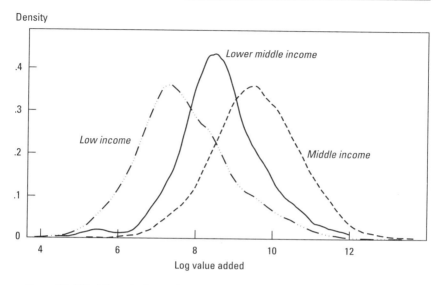

Source: World Bank Enterprise Surveys (www.enterprisesurveys.org).

which captures the dispersion across firms in these countries, is also much greater for the low-income countries and is skewed to the left, indicating that the majority of firms have very low productivity.

Labor productivity, however, is only a partial measure of the productivity and competitiveness of the labor force; workers' wages also need to be considered. If wages are correspondingly low, workers in these countries can still compete with workers in other parts of the world. This issue can be examined by looking at unit labor costs, which measure the ratio of wages to value added and indicate the relative competitiveness of labor across countries. Comparing across countries, we see that almost all countries in Africa are less competitive than China and India (figure 2-19).

However, the competitiveness of labor also captures only a partial picture of productivity, because it does not take into account the amount of machinery and equipment available to each worker and the productivity of capital. To examine the impact of capital and labor on enterprise output differences, we use the OLS regression approach, examining differences in value added across firms after controlling for capital and labor usage and for sectoral differences.

Figure 2-19. Unit Labor Costs

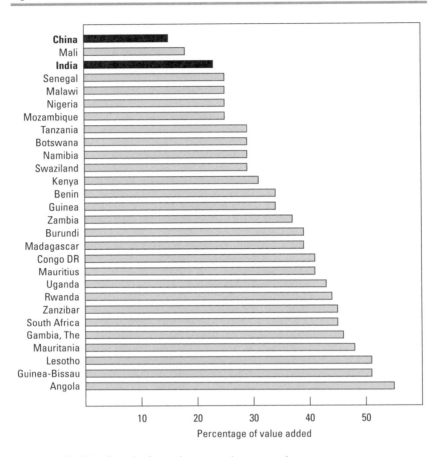

Source: World Bank Enterprise Surveys (www.enterprisesurveys.org).

Differences in the residual, which measures total factor productivity differentials, is presented in figure 2-20, which shows that the productivity of firms in lower-income countries in Africa is much lower than that of firms in middle-income countries such as South Africa, Namibia, and Swaziland.

Total Factor Productivity

We estimate total factor productivity with a model that includes firm-specific characteristics that drive productivity differentials; the results are presented

Figure 2-20. Total Factor Productivity Relative to South Africa

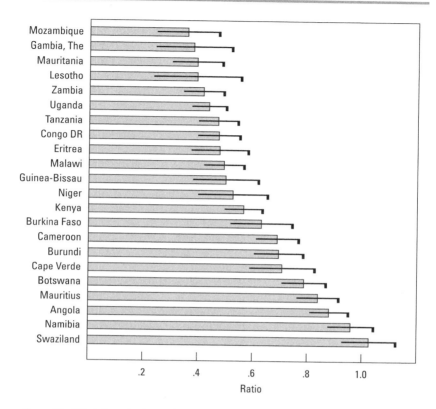

in appendix table A-1.[6] We examine productivity for each income group separately and also control for differences in performance across sectors and countries within each income group. After controlling for these intercept differences, we see that in low-income countries, learning channels such as ISO certification and Internet connections are very significant and positive in determining productivity.

Enterprises that report higher losses due to power outages are not less productive than others, and firms that report higher transport losses—losses due

6. Due to survey limitations, the augmented TFP regressions are estimated for sixteen countries for which we have comparable data.

to breakage or theft—are in fact more productive than others, ceteris paribus. Those results seem counterintuitive, but closer examination of the data shows that firms that face higher demand for their products in low-income environments are more likely to report transport and electricity outages; these firms also are the more productive firms. As expected, having a generator (a sensible precaution) endogenizes the problem—firms that have generators are likely to be more productive than others. For lower-middle-income countries, in which demand is more predictable, firms reporting higher sales losses due to power outages are likely to be less productive and those with generators more productive than others, ceteris paribus.

For middle-income countries in Africa, where there are many fewer power outages, the dispersion is lower and the productivity of firms that report higher outages is no different from that of others. However, in those countries, firms that secure a more reliable power supply by using generators are likely to be more productive than others, indicating the importance of substitute power in overcoming the power shortage problem.[7]

Finally, we turn to the interaction of market structure and firm performance. An adverse business environment might not only affect productivity but also skew the market structure toward firms that can offset their losses with higher revenues resulting from market share advantages, political connections, or better coping mechanisms. As a result, firms with greater market power might suffer more delays and costlier regulation but nevertheless survive because they do not have to compete with other firms.

It is difficult to tease out the effect of market structure from the Enterprise Survey data. In a few countries, questions on influence peddling were included (unfortunately, that is no longer the case). Anecdotal evidence suggests that African manufacturing firms have continued to retain their market leadership in domestic markets by investing in their relationship with governments, thereby maintaining high barriers to entry and reduced competition. Analysis of the Enterprise Survey data confirms that assessment. Comparisons with selected countries in Asia show that lobbying in East Africa is different from lobbying in Asia—in East Africa, larger firms and firms with

---

7. It is important to note that the results described above show correlations between different variables and productivity; they do not show causation. Without time-series data, it is not possible to push our conclusions any further. At this point, they are indicative of the key drivers of business performance and worthy of much more investigation as multiple rounds of survey data become available. Nonetheless, the results do show that total factor productivity is correlated with country-level variables as well as with firm characteristics and various aspects of the business environment.

Table 2-4. Enterprises Lobbying Government and Market Share

Country	Percentage of enterprises lobbying government	Number of enterprises lobbying government	Mean self-reported market share of lobbying enterprises	Mean self-reported market share of non-lobbying enterprises
Senegal	8.3	21	36.8	37.2
Mali	3.9	3	33.2	25.7
Tanzania	13.4	35	31.9	17.9
Uganda	16.4	49	32.7	20.2
Kenya	35.4	97	32	15
Zambia	43.7	90	38	27.7

Source: Ramachandran, Shah, and Tata (2007).

higher market share lobby; in Asia, market share is not a significant determinant of lobbying activity.

Table 2-4 looks at mean self-reported market share and at how many firms acknowledge that they invest in their relationship with the government by lobbying. Firms were asked directly whether they themselves lobby the government to influence the content of laws and regulations that affect their business; lobbying activities included the seeking of special arrangements that would raise the profitability of the enterprise, such as exemptions on tariffs and taxes, quicker clearance at land or sea ports, access to land or other resources, and sole source contracts.

The first striking conclusion is the very high level of self-reported market share. Table 2-4 shows that a limited number of enterprises control market share in many African domestic markets. That finding is likely a reflection of the sparseness of economic activity: even relatively small firms see themselves as having a high share of the domestic market. In most cases, market share controlled by lobbying enterprises is even higher than that reported by enterprises that do not lobby the government.

Is the degree of influence peddling greater in Africa than elsewhere? Most likely it is not—there is a great deal of evidence to suggest a high level of lobbying activity in East Asia and elsewhere (Amsden 1989). The more interesting difference is in self-reported market share. Available data for East Asia show that there is a significant difference between the self-reported market share of lobbying firms in Asia and those in Africa. While firms that lobby in Africa report that they control more than one-third of the market for their main product in the country in which they operate, Asian firms report their share to be just over one-tenth of their far larger, denser, markets. This area needs further investigation—it may be that Asian firms lobby for things like export licenses while African firms lobby to retain domestic market share.

The relationships among market structure, the business environment, the capacity of individual firms, and the performance of firms across different levels of income will be easier to untangle as time-series data become available. The simple approach that we take indicates that the business environment does drive productivity in some areas but that other factors also may play a role in determining outcomes for firms. In the next chapter, we discuss a related set of issues that may shed additional light on the questions raised here, including ownership and entrepreneurial and managerial capability and the question of why there are so few large black-owned businesses in Africa. Understanding these issues as well as the business environment helps us understand the political economy of the private sector in many African countries and what real reform needs to look like.

three

Black Ownership of Businesses in Africa

There are many thousands of black-owned firms in Africa, but few of them are formal, registered firms and even fewer are medium-size or large businesses. The vast majority of black-owned firms are very small businesses with fewer than ten employees. Many of these firms can be described as informal, operating on the margins of the private sector with very little working capital or other resources. The formal business sector, on the other hand, is dominated by medium-size and large businesses, often owned by ethnic minorities. These firms produce the vast majority of value added. It is this phenomenon that we consider in this chapter.

Several similarities were found to exist among fourteen African countries in which questions regarding the ethnic identity of a firm were asked in a consistent way. Of the countries—Angola, Botswana, Burundi, the Democratic Republic of Congo, the Gambia, Guinea-Bissau, Guinea, Kenya, Mauritania, Namibia, Rwanda, Swaziland, Tanzania, and Uganda—most, if not all, had been colonized by European countries. Almost all pursued a postindependence industrialization strategy that focused on import substitution and the creation of a large state-owned sector. That in turn led to the emergence of an inefficient, dualistic manufacturing sector, in which a large number of informal and small firms coexisted with a few relatively large, capital-intensive businesses. Some countries, such as Tanzania, adopted socialist policies that sought to marginalize the business class; others, such as Angola,

Burundi, and Uganda, experienced devastating civil wars or dictatorial rule that severely disrupted normal business development.

Most of the countries also adopted World Bank–initiated structural adjustment programs in the 1980s or 1990s to reform their economies and pursue outward-oriented growth. However, as discussed below, their manufacturing sectors remain small and fragmented—the majority of manufacturing remains under the control of either the state or ethnic minority groups, which account for much of the employment generation in non-extractive industries in the formal private sector. Understanding why black-owned firms in the formal private sector tend to be small is important because further broad-based growth of manufacturing can occur only with the participation of domestic businesses, including those of the indigenous majority.

Indigenous and Minority-Owned Firms in the Formal Private Sector

The discussion that follows is based on survey data for the fourteen African countries in which questions regarding ethnic identity of the firm were asked consistently. We use the data to identify key characteristics of *indigenous* (black African–owned) firms in the formal private sector. It is important at this point to define "indigenous" and "minority-owned." "Indigenous" refers to firms that are black African–owned, including those that are run by owner-entrepreneurs, those with black African majority shareholders, and those that are owned by black Africans from a country in Africa other than the one in which the business is located. "Minority-owned" refers to firms that are owned by individuals or shareholders who are not black African but are African nationals of Asian, Caucasian, or Middle Eastern descent. Minority firms that are foreign-owned include firms whose owners are, for example, from Europe or Asia and who do not have African citizenship; foreign-owned minority firms also are included in our definition of "minority-owned."

The distribution of indigenous and minority-owned firms in our sample shows that many of the firms are in fact indigenous (figure 3-1), but we can also see that the relatively small share of minority-owned firms controls the vast majority of value added (figure 3-2). Except in three countries—Angola, Guinea-Bissau, and Swaziland—minority-owned firms control *50 percent or more* of value added in industry. In Guinea, Tanzania, and Kenya, they control more than 80 percent of value added.

The size distribution (as measured by number of employees) in our sample also is revealing. Figure 3-3, which gives the start-up and current size of

Figure 3-1. Distribution of Firms in Manufacturing, by Ethnicity[a]

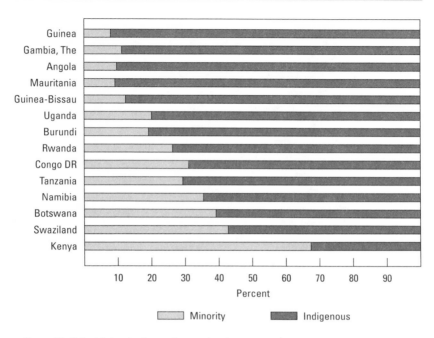

Source: World Bank Enterprise Surveys (www.enterprisesurveys.org).
a. Weighted frequency.

indigenous and minority-owned firms, shows that indigenous firms entered the market at significantly smaller sizes than minority-owned businesses. While the average firm size at start-up of minority-owned firms in Tanzania was about sixty employees, the number was just under twenty for indigenous businesses. For most countries, minority firms started at a size that was two to three times greater than that of indigenous businesses.

We also see that the difference in size persisted over time—size at the time of the survey did not differ much from size at start-up for indigenous businesses. In Uganda, for example, there was virtually no difference between the current size of indigenous firms and their size when they started—in other words, there had been virtually no growth. In some countries, a wide gap emerges over time between indigenous and minority entrepreneurs. Data on the age of firms surveyed (not reported here) show that minority-owned firms are not all that much older than indigenous businesses; therefore it is

Figure 3-2. Distribution of Value Added, by Ethnicity

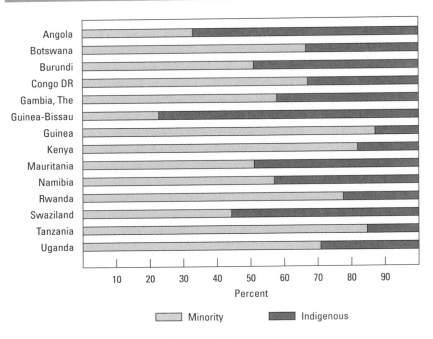

Source: World Bank Enterprise Surveys (www.enterprisesurveys.org).

not that they are bigger because they have been around longer. Over roughly the same period, minority firms were simply able to grow at a faster rate in many countries in Africa. The size differential between minority and indigenous firms at the time of survey was close to ten in Uganda, four in Tanzania, six in Rwanda, ten in Guinea, and almost five in Angola.

It is not easy to separate out the productivity effects of ownership because of the strong correlation with size. As seen in the previous chapter, larger firms tend to have higher productivity than small firms across the sample of countries surveyed. Larger firms are also far more likely to be minority owned. Size picks up much of the differential in capabilities, access to networks, and other factors that reflect ownership. Consequently, it is difficult to identify the impact of ownership on productivity. However, we are able to identify the differences in the growth rates of black-owned and minority firms and to investigate the reasons for those differences.

Figure 3-3. Start-up and Current Size of Indigenous and Minority-Owned Firms

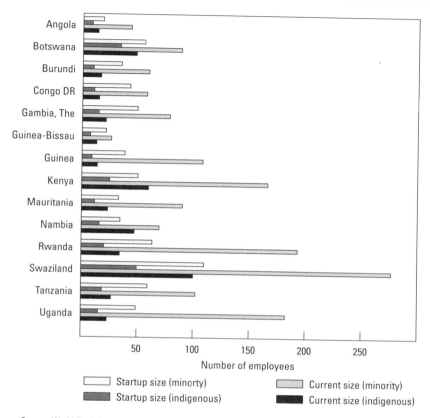

Source: World Bank Enterprise Surveys (www.enterprisesurveys.org).

Do some black-owned firms grow faster than others? Owners' attainment of a university education was very important in determining the size of the firm (figure 3-4). We also observe that indigenous entrepreneurs with a university education started much larger firms than those that did not have a university degree in almost all of the countries surveyed.[1] University education

1. There are other analyses of the role of ethnicity in the private sector in Africa. Most notable is Taye Mengistae (2001), which looks at the role of ethnicity in the indigenous private sector in Ethiopia. More recently, Fafchamps (2004) examines the dynamics of the private sector, including the role of ethnicity, in a comprehensive analysis of markets in sub-Saharan Africa.

Figure 3-4. Average Current Firm Size, by Education of the Owner

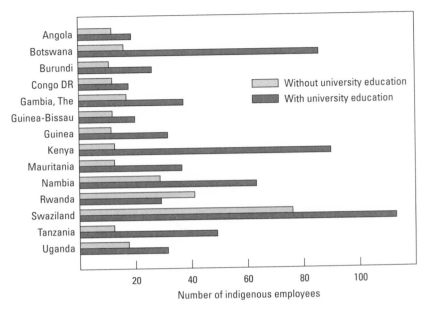

Source: World Bank Enterprise Surveys (www.enterprisesurveys.org).

appears to be correlated with a larger size at start-up and a higher rate of growth for black-owned businesses.[2]

There are three possible interpretations of the finding regarding the impact of university education: a university education provides an owner with the tools to run a firm; completion of a university degree reflects greater ability on the part of an owner and consequently greater potential for success of a firm; and a university degree enables an owner to access a network of other professionals who provide information or facilitates access to credit. This finding is worthy of further investigation to indentify which of those factors is driving our results.

Do indigenous firms have less access to credit? That is the key question. Are they less likely to have bank accounts, overdraft protection, and loans? Is

2. Not reported here is the gap for minority firms according to educational attainment. This gap is much smaller; not being university-educated is less of a disadvantage for this group in starting and building a business.

Figure 3-5. Firms with Overdraft Protection, by Ethnicity

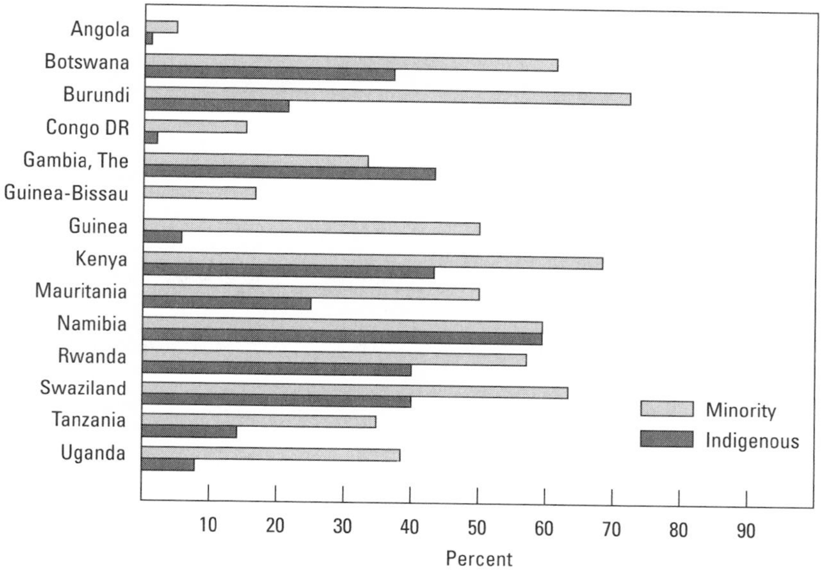

Source: World Bank Enterprise Surveys (www.enterprisesurveys.org).

access to the banking sector correlated with financial depth? Or are banks simply sorting firms according to their creditworthiness? In almost all the countries in our sample, we see that indigenous firms have less access to overdraft protection than minority-owned firms (figure 3-5).[3]

But the data also present evidence suggesting that the financial sector sorts firms to determine their creditworthiness. Figure 3-6 shows that there also are big differences in the percent of firms with audited accounts when disaggregated by ethnicity. Similarly, indigenous firms are less likely than minority-owned firms to own their business premises; consequently, they have less collateral with which to obtain financing (figure 3-7). These firms are less likely to be creditworthy and so have less access to finance.

---

3. Access to loans follows a pattern similar to that for overdrafts, but the differences across ethnicity are not pronounced. In fact, in countries such as Botswana, Namibia, Swaziland, and Namibia, *more* indigenous firms than minority firms use loans. It may well be that indigenous firms simply choose to use a different type of financing.

Figure 3-6. Firms with Audited Accounts, by Ethnicity

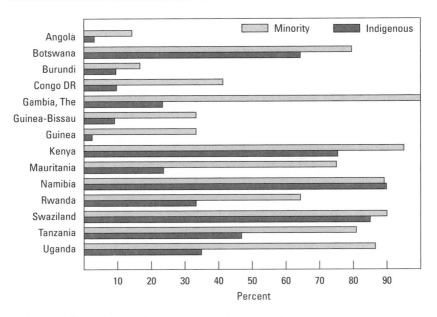

Source: World Bank Enterprise Surveys (www.enterprisesurveys.org).

Supplier Credit

Do indigenous firms have lower access to supplier credit? This type of credit enables the purchase of key inputs with a sixty- or ninety-day payment period. Figure 3-8 presents data on the percentage of firms using supplier credit. In all cases, indigenous firms have less access to supplier credit than do minority-owned firms.

Less access to supplier credit could be related to indigenous firms' age or to lack of a history of business transactions with suppliers—again, lenders may simply be sorting on the basis of creditworthiness rather than engaging in race discrimination. Figure 3-9 shows that firms that used trade credit did have longer relationships with their suppliers than those that did not use trade credit, except for firms in Botswana and Uganda. Overall, the evidence does not point strongly toward discrimination against black-owned firms but more toward the notion that banks do not lend to firms when they are unsure of being repaid.

Figure 3-7. Firms Owning Premises, by Ethnicity

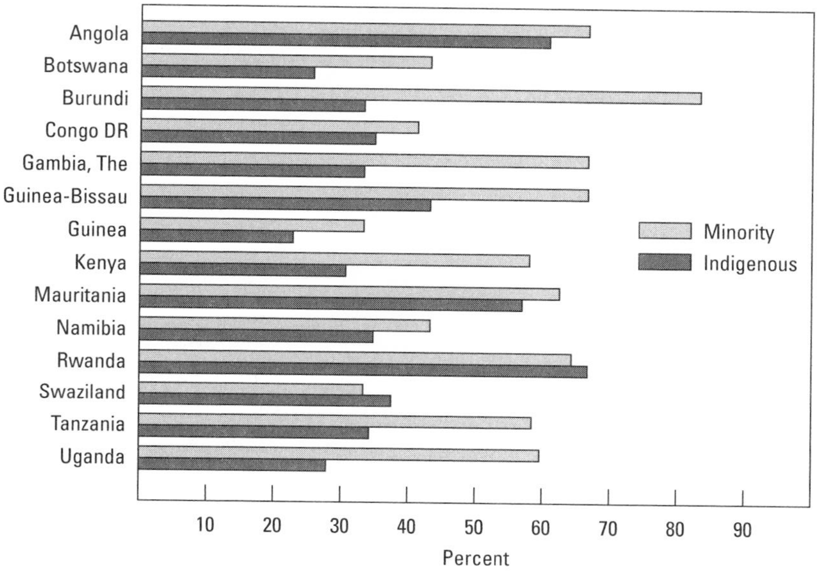

Source: World Bank Enterprise Surveys (www.enterprisesurveys.org).

Determinants of Access to Credit

The descriptive statistics show that indigenous firms have less access to credit than minority firms in some types of financial products but not in others. Indigenous firms also are less creditworthy—they are less likely to have audited accounts and land that can be used as collateral for a loan. However, all of that could be because they generally are younger and smaller. It already has been established that indigenous firms own smaller firms. The banking sector and suppliers could simply be rationing out firms that are less established and that have a higher risk of failure.

We examine these hypotheses by running multivariate probit regressions with access to credit as the dependent variable. The results are presented in appendix 1, table A-2. In all cases, larger firms are much more likely to obtain credit than smaller businesses, ceteris paribus. Firm age is not significant in our estimations.

Indigenous firms also are less likely to have working capital finance such as overdraft protection and trade credit, and that remains true even after the

Figure 3-8. Firms Receiving Supplier Credit, by Ethnicity

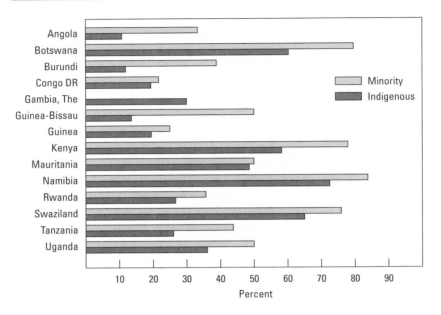

Source: World Bank Enterprise Surveys (www.enterprisesurveys.org).

analysis controls for size and age. However, they are more likely to have bank loans for investment. Having land to use as collateral matters—those owning land are much more likely to have bank loans and overdrafts than others. University education matters, too, particularly for indigenous businesses, for gaining access to working capital finance from banks; managers with higher education are more likely to have overdraft protection than owners without. Surprisingly though, education does not matter for having bank loans, perhaps indicating preferential treatment of indigenous entrepreneurs on the part of banks and other lending institutions.

Overall, our results present a mixed picture—indigenous firms may suffer from less access to credit in some situations, but other explanations also are possible. One is that the financial sector is likely to be sorting firms on the basis of creditworthiness. Another is that the need for credit may differ across firms, rather than access. Our results do point toward the need to establish credit registries and other means of evaluating firms rather than simply focusing on the expansion of the supply of credit.

Figure 3-9. *Average Years of Relationship with Supplier, Indigenous Firms*

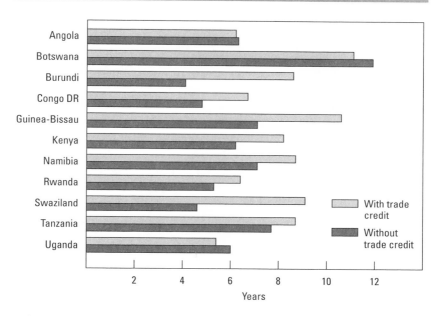

Source: World Bank Enterprise Surveys (www.enterprisesurveys.org).

Why Are Indigenous Firms Lagging in Africa?

An important aspect of the success of firms is their ability to survive and grow. We formulate a simple econometric model that enables us to test hypotheses regarding the determinants of start-up size and firm growth. At this stage, our cross-sectional data do not allow us to develop an identification strategy that would lead to conclusive results on causality. But we can look at *correlations* between firm growth (as measured by number of employees) and variables such as age, size, and owner's educational attainment. We can do this for the entire sample as well as for indigenous and non-indigenous firms separately, as the appropriate statistical test (F test) allows us to break up the sample in this manner. In particular, we look at two key variables—access to overdraft protection and attainment of a university degree—to see whether they are correlated with start-up size and rate of growth. The results are presented in appendix 1, table A-3.

The first set of three regressions looks at the determinants of growth for the whole sample as well as for indigenous and non-indigenous businesses.

The first equation shows that after we control for several factors, indigenous firms have a lower rate of growth. We also see that although secondary education and vocational training are not significant, a university education is significant in determining a firm's growth rate. On disaggregating the sample, we see that the university education variables *are significant only for indigenous businesses*. It may be that university education imparts much-needed skills to operate a firm and to survive exogenous shocks or that it provides access to a network of business professionals who in turn provide access to knowledge, capital, and other inputs necessary for survival and growth.

It is also interesting to note that *indigenous firms of foreign origin* grow faster than those of local origin. In other words, a black African entrepreneur who has moved from Kenya to Tanzania is likely to build his or her firm faster than an entrepreneur operating in his or her own country. It may well be that a businessperson of African origin who can operate across national boundaries is more able or skilled than one who operates only within national borders.

Networks play a critical role in the African private sector. Our data show that the ethnicity of a business owner remains an important determinant of access to credit and a number of other performance variables, even when controls such as owner's education level and title to marketable assets are included in regressions. Usually within ethnic minority communities, networks help firms overcome the limitations of financial markets. At the same time, they effectively exclude outsiders from areas of business. Networks operate in many other regions, including fast-growing Asian countries, where they may have similarly positive effects in enabling their members to compensate for dysfunctional market institutions. But their overall impact is likely to be different in Asia and Africa, because of differences in economic density and market size. In Asia, their adverse effect in stifling competition is likely to be small because of the competitive pressure that results from having many firms that belong to many networks. However, in Africa's very small economies, the adverse effect of a few dominant networks or firms is likely to be far greater. Firms in sparse economies are likely to give more weight to the costs and risks of encouraging entry through reforms than are firms in dense economies.

Small, sparse industrial sectors dominated by a few, often ethnically segmented, firms with high market share are therefore likely to see less dynamic competition. The greater access of larger, networked firms to technology, credit, and business expertise creates rents that, even if shared with government, would be dissipated by more open entry. That can reduce the incentive to push hard for better regulation and business services. As discussed above, the segmented nature of many African business communities can complicate the process of developing effective means of communication between the business and government sectors to improve the business environment. At the same time, the prominent role of minority and expatriate firms increases the public's reservations over the market economy model, including large privatizations. The danger is a low-level equilibrium with high costs, limited pressure for reform from the business community and the public, and limited response from government.

Africa is not the only region where indigenous participation in larger-scale businesses lags behind that of some ethnic groups or foreign investors. Similar situations prevail in parts of Latin America, the Andean countries in particular, while concern in Malaysia over the level of indigenous participation in commercial agriculture and modern industry and commerce has been an important factor shaping policies there. Foreign investments in "sensitive" sectors have also been a matter of political controversy in the United States. In many African countries, firm surveys indicate that indigenous black-owned firms lag behind minority-owned firms and foreign-owned firms on a number of dimensions, including size and the rate of growth.

From the narrowly economic perspective, ownership patterns may not seem to be vital. But from the broader perspective of political economy, the issue is clearly of considerable concern. First, to the extent that ownership imbalances reflect inequitable barriers to participation, the economy loses the benefits of widespread access to opportunity. Second, as recognized in many countries, including Malaysia and South Africa, severe imbalances in the patterns of ownership and perceived wealth and power have the potential to encourage populist policies that can derail development. At best, ownership imbalances can generate a climate of mutual suspicion between government and a large part of the business community, which undermines the confidence to invest; at worst, such imbalances can lead to xenophobia and the expulsion of economically important minorities, with dire consequences for the economy as a whole. The domination of the business sector by a few large businesses, usually minority or expatriate owned, in countries with low economic density helps to sustain the ambivalent public attitude toward private sector–led development that has been noted, for example, in Afrobarometer surveys (Bratton, Mattes, and Gyimah-Boadi 2005). The danger lies in settling for a "low-level political equilibrium" with marginal reforms, leaving Africa falling further behind the rest of the world.

A clearer understanding of why indigenous firms often lag behind those owned by minority and foreign interests is therefore important in understanding the reasons behind the structure of business groups in Africa and the resulting political economy of reforms. We know that markets are thin and that the sparseness of economic activity results in the persistence of one dominant network in most countries. We also know that overall, the business environment is difficult, imposing high costs and risks on all businesses. Some may be better able to cope with certain difficulties than others. For example, in the face of unreliable power, larger firms with greater resources are more likely to be able to afford generators than smaller businesses. Certain large firms may also be more able to make special arrangements to protect themselves from predation. Yet at the same time, evidence from firm surveys suggests that often larger firms are also more vulnerable to failures in the business environment than small businesses. They transact over longer distances, are more dependent on sophisticated logistics, and are less able to operate under the radar of official scrutiny.

Overall, the evidence does not support the thesis that ownership imbalances are simply the result of an asymmetric business environment for indigenous and minority- and foreign-owned businesses, although social features of certain minority groups, in particular their ability to network to support "clusters" of related businesses, may assist them in overcoming some of the constraints of a poor business environment. The data support a more complex thesis—that the interaction of a high-cost business environment, a low-density economic environment, and the dominance of minority-owned businesses may underlie the absence of a broad-based private sector in many African countries.

Some Africa scholars argue that it is convenient to have a private sector that is dominated by ethnic minorities, who do not pose a significant threat to political power and often provide a steady stream of rents. The minority Asian community in East Africa, which has thrived even in difficult times, often coexists with a small, wealthy, indigenous private sector, and both are closely aligned with the president or his associates (Tangri 1999). The survival of this group depends on its political connections and rent-sharing arrangements with the government. The government in turn relies on it for extra-budgetary revenues. Other scholars reinforce this perspective, arguing that the political elite in Africa have found mechanisms by which to preserve rent-seeking arrangements with the help of a small private sector enclave (van de Walle 2001). When faced with donor country–driven reforms, governments often have reacted by accomplishing partial reform, thereby satisfying the rich countries, while preserving rent-seeking arrangements (van de Walle 2001). As a result, there has not been much change in the structure or competitiveness of the private sector. Indeed, reforms often have increased the level of uncertainty for the business community more than anything else.

On the whole, relatively little research has been done on the factors responsible for the imbalances in the business environment, and any conclusions on their causes are somewhat speculative. However, we present three possible explanations: culture and the ability to network, history, and risk diversification. We recognize that this is an area that requires further research.

Culture and the ability to network. Evidence suggests that many clusters of minority-owned firms belong to networks that usually are based on trust between members of a relatively small minority group and that can help firms overcome the limitations of a poor business environment (Fafchamps 2004). The data on access to finance do not suggest that black-owned firms are denied access to credit; instead, they indicate that firms of all races are sorted according to creditworthiness. However, Biggs and Shah (2006) show that the ethnicity of business proprietors remains an important determinant of access to credit and a number of other performance variables even when other dimensions, such as the education level of proprietors and title to marketable assets, are included as explanatory variables.

At the same time, networks effectively exclude outsiders from many areas of business. Networks operate in many other regions, including fast-growing Asian countries, but their overall impact is likely to be different in Asia and Africa because of differences in economic density and market size. In Asia, their stifling effect on competition is likely to be small because of the competitive pressure generated by having many firms belonging to many networks. However, in Africa's very small economies, the adverse effect of a few dominant networks or firms is likely to be far larger. Dominant firms in sparse economies are likely to give more weight to the risk that reforms may encourage entry than are firms in dense economies; as a result, they are less likely to lobby aggressively for reform.

Indigenous value systems do not always encourage investment, wealth-creation, and risk taking (Platteau and Hayami 1998). Some value systems embody a strong ethic of sharing, placing heavy obligations on successful members to share gains with other members of the group. Platteau and Hayami argue that in land-abundant societies (more likely to be in Africa), the sharing of assets and income other than land is more significant than in societies that are land-scarce (in Asia). They pose detailed theories on how resources are shared and how people who do not conform to social norms are punished. They also discuss attitudes toward wealth and argue that many African societies stress egalitarianism over the accumulation of wealth by individuals. Other researchers argue that norms regarding wealth sharing may lead to a disincentive to migrate from a village to a town to become an urban worker or entrepreneur. Kinship, they argue, can be viewed as a poverty trap (Hoff and Sen 2006).

History. During the colonial period and at independence, most larger-scale agriculture, industry, and commerce were in the hands of minority and expatriate investors. One of the consequences, in many countries, was a wave of indigenization and nationalization that was reversed in the course of the 1990s. Few countries, therefore, have grown strong indigenous business communities that are accustomed to operating in a competitive market environment.

Risk diversification. Firm surveys find that higher education of the owner is one of the predictors of business success for indigenous businesses but that relatively few owners and managers of indigenous firms have had access to higher education. Faced with highly unstable and uncertain politics and economies, many of Africa's educated elite have migrated outside the region (Ndulu and O'Connell 2006).

In contrast, investment in Africa's economies by minorities and foreign investors often is part of an investor's multicountry investment and risk-diversification strategy. Increasingly, these investors include black investors from other African countries and sometimes black Africans who have immigrated to other countries. Survey results suggest that firms owned by such investors are little different from those owned by other foreign investors. This supports the view that the issue is not race per se; it is instead the range of opportunities and capabilities possessed by different groups and the impact of culture in helping firms surmount some of the difficulties posed by the business environment.

four

Approaches to Building Africa's Private Sector

Today, countries like Uganda are still 90% unserved by electricity. Can you imagine not having power in 90% of any country and still trying to grow the economy? Do we expect Africans to wait for grid electricity to incrementally reach people or are there disruptive innovations that can provide off-grid renewable energy to rural Africans in scaleable ways? What would this look like given large geo-thermal and bio-diesel reserves in East Africa and can renewable energy sources provide opportunities for greener solutions in Africa? Interacting with dynamic and bright Africans under 30 (who make up 70% or more of most African countries), I cannot help but wonder what is on the horizon. People are innovating all over the continent with bio-gas, small scale hydro, wind, and solar power. Where people have electricity, there is a massive difference in economic activity, public services, productivity, and hope about the future. Energy is truly a platform that affects nearly every aspect of rural life. Today, Africa is mostly unserved by power grids but given innovation possibilities, are there not scalable ways to introduce renewable energy to millions of people who are completely unplugged from the global economy today?

ALEEM WALJI, *from the Google.org blog, July 9, 2008*

Enterprise surveys conducted in many African countries point to a number of constraints that are slowing the emergence of vibrant, competitive business sectors. Most obvious and immediate is the need to improve the poor quality of infrastructure services, power especially but also transport. Also important are two other issues: the need to overcome the constraints imposed by small, sparse national markets with limited competition and the need to broaden the base of the private sector. Low competition and the split of many national business sectors along the twin dimensions of size and productivity and ethnicity complicate the political economy of reform, making it less likely that governments and business will form unified fronts to push for better business services, greater openness, and more competition.

The problems are real, but there is room for optimism as well. On the infrastructure side, advancing technology, partly impelled by concern about climate change, holds out special promise for Africa. So do new approaches toward project finance, including public-private partnerships and approaches based on regional cooperation. In terms of policy, African leaders are more pro-business than before, and they are eager to get away from aid dependence and donor conditionality. The private sector in Africa has a stronger voice as well—for example, it is now more common to see private sector representatives at consultative meetings with rich country aid organizations. More African leaders and members of cabinets are being drawn from the private sector, and the concerns of this new generation, such as high levels of unemployment, poverty, and dependence on foreign aid, are different from those of their predecessors who were more concerned with independence, statehood, and the maintenance of power (Emery 2003). Moreover, businesses based in African countries are beginning to invest across borders, creating a potential constituency that can be helpful to drive initiatives for regional integration.

Another reason to be optimistic is the rising technocratic class in sub-Saharan Africa that is well aware of the challenges to raising income and competing globally, including infrastructure investments, regulations, and maintenance. This is not the Africa of the 1970s and 1980s when many infrastructure projects failed because of poor design and lack of capacity to regulate and maintain services. Most countries in Africa have undergone macroeconomic reforms and have inflation under control. Many non-resource-rich countries have been enjoying high growth rates for over a decade (Gelb, Ramachandran, and Turner 2007), and some, such as Ghana, are now able to borrow from commercial markets. Central banks and finance ministries are run now largely by very competent, highly trained individuals. In several countries, democratically elected leaders have searched the world to bring the best talent back to their countries.

Plugging the Infrastructure Gap: Clean Energy, Better Roads, and Regional Cooperation

The evidence on the constraints as seen by businesses discussed in chapter 2 points overwhelmingly to the need to invest in infrastructure. In particular, a steady and reliable supply of electricity is hard to come by in many countries.[1]

Conventional energy investments will continue to be vital to sustain growth in Africa. But the continent also has a unique opportunity to lead the way for the rest of the world—to become a producer (and even an exporter) of energy with zero net emissions of greenhouse gases, notably hydroelectric and solar power. Countries in Africa can avoid the predicament that some rapidly growing countries now find themselves in—rising incomes accompanied by a high incidence of ill health and respiratory disease caused by severe air and water pollution.

Africa has tremendous potential for the production of various kinds of renewable energy (OECD 2003/2004). African reserves of renewable resources are the highest in the world (Buys and others 2007), and many countries have a potential for solar, wind, hydro, and biofuel generation that greatly exceeds their total energy consumption. Buys and colleagues list the top thirty-five countries in the world that have the biggest total reserves of solar, wind, hydro, and geothermal energy—the set includes seventeen countries in sub-Saharan Africa. Of the top thirty-five countries, Africa also has twenty-one for solar energy, six for wind, eleven for hydro, and seven for geothermal. Buys and colleagues show that Africa has renewable energy reserves to meet its future needs and possibly the needs of other parts of the world, including Europe.

Much of sub-Saharan Africa receives solar radiation of the order of 6–8 kilowatt-hours (kWh) per meter squared per day—some of the highest levels of solar radiation in the world. For firms now paying upward of 15 to 20 cents per kWh for electricity that is unreliable and of low quality, the installation of solar panels can reduce reliance upon poorly maintained grids and would lower costs, which in turn would enable them to compete more effectively in the global market. Solar energy generated via rooftop panels is

---

1. Macroeconomic analyses of the returns to infrastructure also confirm the importance of a reliable supply of power and roads (Munnell 1992; Calderon and Servén 2004; Demurger 2001; Canning and Pedroni 1999). The lack of infrastructure has also been shown to have negative impacts on intra-African trade, shrinking cross-country and cross-regional flows to a fraction of their potential levels (Limao and Venables 1999).

Figure 4-1. Solar: Annual Average Latitude Tilt Map at 40 km Resolution for Africa[a]

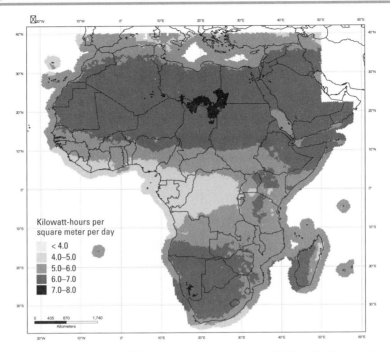

Source: Adapted from Solar and Wind Energy Resource Assessment (SWERA) of the United Nations Environment Programme (UNEP) and National Renewable Energy Laboratory (NREL) of the U.S. Department of Energy, Office of Energy Efficiency and Renewable Energy, 2005 (http://swera.unep.net/typo3conf/ext/metadata_tool/archive/download/africatilt_218.pdf).

a. The latitude tilt measurement of solar radiation is the total radiation (sun plus sky and clouds) falling on a flat plate that is angled from the ground toward the sun equal to the latitude. The sun is closer to being perpendicular to the plate during parts of the year, and the overall solar resource is somewhat higher than the "global horizontal" data and likely to be the most relevant for our purposes.

also less problematic in terms of the regulation and management issues that have plagued delivery of grid-based energy by public utilities. Figure 4-1 shows the solar radiation and solar energy potential of the African continent. In a 2007 article, the *Economist* argues that solar energy will become cost effective in Africa if costs are lowered by 30 percent.[2]

Some types of renewable energies are the most cost-effective solutions right now, according to a publication from the Energy Sector Management Assistance Program (ESMAP) of the World Bank (World Bank 2006a). Given

2. "The Dark Continent," *Economist*, August 16, 2007.

its title, "Technical and Economic Assessment of Off-Grid, Mini-Grid and Grid Electrification Technologies," this report does not exactly jump off the shelf. But it has particularly important implications for the private sector in Africa. The good news in the report is that for much of Africa, where millions of people have yet to be connected to a power grid, renewable energy may well be the cheapest option. The report carefully costs out a variety of power generation technologies that range from 50 watts to 500 megawatts (MW) and that include renewable energy technologies (such as photovoltaic, wind, geothermal, hydro, biomass-electric, and biogas-electric) as well as conventional generation technologies. The costing exercise was conducted for three periods—2005, 2010, and 2015—incorporating uncertainty and sensitivity analyses around key assumptions. It concluded that renewable energy is more economical than conventional energy for off-grid generation of less than 5 kW—exactly the sort of power currently needed by almost half of the 500 million people who do not have access to modern energy. Renewable energy is also potentially the cheapest source of power for mini-grid generation. Conventional power generation still holds the advantage for large-scale needs, but for much of sub-Saharan Africa, it is off-grid and mini-grid generation that is necessary to meet the needs of a sparsely distributed population and to enable businesses to widen their geographic spread, especially the smaller businesses that are unable to absorb the costs of generator power.

New research also shows that baseload-scale solar thermal power is now lower cost than high-efficiency coal-fired power, at a carbon dioxide emissions charge below the level that is set by the European Union's new climate action plan, and far below the level recommended by the Stern Review (Wheeler 2008). Using carbon charges to guide project selection is increasingly feasible, because new bilateral and multilateral clean technology funds are available to finance the incremental cost gap between dirty and clean power. The World Bank has recently launched a Clean Technology Fund, for which the United States, the United Kingdom, and Japan have already pledged several billion dollars. This fund must always focus on major shifts toward clean energy as opposed to changes at the margin. In the medium to long term, clean energy funds would have to grow tenfold in scale to handle the emissions problem globally: the International Energy Agency estimates that $30 billion annually will be required to close the incremental cost gap between clean and conventional energy investments. Africa should position itself to benefit from the opportunities created by such funds.

Firms in rich countries are increasingly engaged in research and development of a vast array of newer, cleaner sources of power, much of which can be transferred to Africa. Exciting new developments include hydro, wind power, and biofuels, such as oil from the jatropha plant. Micro hydro projects in Africa are now providing electricity for several hundred households each, bringing modern energy to far-flung areas. In Kenya, the community-owned Tungu-Kabiri Micro Hydro project, located in Mbuiru, supplies 18 kW of power and has 200 shareholders, each of whom has bought shares in the enterprise.[3] On an even smaller scale, pico hydro schemes that typically supply power up to 5 kW are also proving to be good value. In two towns in the Kirinyaga district in Kenya, very small-scale hydro units (so called micro hydro and pico hydro) are providing power to about sixty households each, while substantially reducing the use of kerosene and biomass fuels (Television Trust for the Environment 2002). These options are extremely relevant for a continent where it is likely that the costs of expanding traditional grid-based electricity will limit its spread to sparsely populated areas.

Dozens of firms in the United States and Europe, fueled by venture capital investments, are engaged in research and development to bring down the cost of such renewable energy alternatives. Venture capital activity in solar energy increased almost fourfold, from $59 million in 2004 to $308 million in 2006.[4] The U.S. government's interest in the development of alternative energies, in addition to legislated emissions reductions, is creating demand that investors see as a major incentive for investments in renewable energy sources.[5] Solar efficiency has increased dramatically since the 1970s, with accompanying declines in costs. The goal of the U.S. Department of Energy is to make the cost of solar power competitive with the grid by 2015, and many in the field think that that is a conservative target.[6] Some companies in the United States and Australia are trying to build large-scale plants that will store and supply base-load power on a twenty-four-hour basis at competitive prices. Appendix 2 lists some of the venture capital–funded efforts in the United States and other rich countries that are focused on solar energy.

Rich countries can use incentives such as tax credits to lower the risks of technological development, speed up the production of clean technologies, and facilitate contact between solar energy developers and relevant partners in Africa. For example, the Overseas Private Investment Corporation (OPIC)

---

3. For more information about this and other hydro power projects, see Practical Action's website (www.practicalaction.org/?id=region_east_africa_energy).

4. "Bright Prospects," *Economist*, March 8, 2007, citing Cleantech Venture Network.

5. Twenty-five states plus the District of Columbia have binding clean energy standards. California's recent greenhouse law requires the state to reduce its overall emissions by 25 percent by 2020.

6. "Bright Prospects," *Economist*, March 8, 2007.

has a strong tradition of providing support to the private sector and can play a key role. In 2007 OPIC launched a program to reduce emissions from OPIC-supported projects and to support projects that are focused on energy efficiency and clean technology. OPIC has also announced the creation of a private equity investment fund—the Catalyst Private Equity Fund—with a target capitalization of $100 million to invest in projects in the water and clean energy sector in the Middle East and North Africa. That type of market-driven mechanism can be expanded to sub-Saharan Africa, where it can be combined with risk insurance and financing to firms investing in the development and provision of clean energy. In general, aid institutions can play a key role, monitoring new developments in solar, wind, and hydro power; facilitating the transfer of new technologies; and funding start-up and other costs in bringing these technologies to Africa.

Large-scale hydropower projects also have the potential to meet a significant share of Africa's power needs. These projects continue to generate controversy because of environmental and governance concerns, but there are new best practice models that can be relied on to mitigate negative effects. Several hydropower projects are currently under consideration or at the early stages of development in Uganda, Ethiopia, and elsewhere that have the potential to address Africa's energy crisis. In 2007 the African Development Bank commissioned a feasibility study for Grand Inga. It is the most ambitious of all and seeks to vastly expand Africa's power generation capacity by harnessing the Inga Falls on the Congo River. Inga sends 42.5 million liters of water pouring into the Atlantic Ocean every second—a flow volume that is second only to the Amazon. It is estimated that Grand Inga will cost upwards of $40 billion and generate up to 39,000 MW of electric power, supplying the needs of many African firms and households and even possibly those in Europe and the Middle East.[7]

No approach is without its concerns, however. One is the risk of increasing countries' dependence on hydropower during an era of drought and unreliable rainfall induced by climate change. But water storage capacity is grossly underexploited and estimated to be only about 5 percent of potential storage levels. Increased capacity can provide considerable potential for hydropower even in areas of variable rainfall.

Issues of governance have also been of concern in the delivery of large-scale projects. In recent years, energy projects have had to deal with charges

---

7. John Reed, "The Inga Hydroelectric Plant: Coincidence Inspires Hope," *Financial Times*, November 20, 2006. p.4.

of bribery and corruption. Multilateral institutions and individual countries have taken action against large firms, albeit in a somewhat piecemeal fashion. Ironically, these efforts have led to the exit of some large firms that are capable of delivering large infrastructure projects. In 2003 the world's largest power-producing company, AES, pulled out of the Bujagali Falls project, resulting in delays that have left much of Uganda with rolling blackouts of 8 to 10 hours per day (Environment News Service 2003). AES's decision was driven in part by economic reasons, but the company also fell victim to problems of corruption; in 2003 it was alleged that AES paid, or agreed to pay, bribes in violation of the U.S. Foreign Corrupt Practices Act. In addition, the original contract between AES and the government of Uganda was kept secret; when legal action forced the document to become public, civic organizations complained that the payments to AES would have been greatly in excess of what would be considered fair compensation.

Similar fates have befallen Lahmeyer International GmbH, a major infrastructure company operating in several countries around the world, and Acres International, a Canadian enterprise specializing in infrastructure (World Bank 2006b, Bretton Woods Project 2004). Both companies are large and capable of delivering major infrastructure projects. Between 2002 and 2003, both were convicted of bribery and corruption charges in Lesotho. Several more construction and engineering firms from the United States, the United Kingdom, Canada, and Japan currently appear on the World Bank's list of debarred businesses. Many firms capable of delivering on large-scale infrastructure projects either are wary about bidding on projects in Africa or are already on the list of debarred businesses. This reduces the number of firms that can bid on any given project and therefore means less competition in the construction sector.

The management of large-scale projects by national governments raises a number of governance-related issues, including tendering and procurement processes, the collection of tolls, and contracts for maintenance of roads and power plants. Some may be pessimistic about the capacity of African governments to manage these administrative functions well. However, new best practice models are available to governments and investors (such as the Nam Theun 2 hydroelectric power project in Laos) as well as a vast amount of technical capacity from multilateral institutions such as the World Bank and the African Development Bank. In addition, moving to a regionally cooperative project base could secure a degree of separation from national political pressures and so help in containing corruption. It may seem that national governments lose a degree of sovereignty in regional investment projects that are backed with large amounts of international funding. But it is important to keep in mind the benefits that come with these projects—good project design using the lessons of best practice can create layers of safeguards as well as more transparent and rigorous methods of procurement, distribution, maintenance, and pricing of services. Agreed tariff policies should be implemented vigorously, and competitive bidding, in the most transparent manner possible, must be the focus of all infrastructure projects.

Concerns about resettlement due to the loss of homes and farmland and the destruction of environmental assets, including the loss of habitat for wildlife, are indeed serious. But they can be addressed by consultative processes, involvement of community organizations at every stage of design and construction, and external monitoring by relevant agencies. The Nam Theun 2 project serves as a good example of this process.[8] On the basis of an extensive, multiyear consultative process, this 1,070 MW hydropower project has a number of environmental and social safeguards to protect the people affected by the project and to preserve the biodiversity in the area (Asian Development Bank 2007). Although not based in Africa, the Nam Theun 2 project can serve as an important model of learning from outside the region, especially for the design and planning process for large-scale infrastructure development. Governance and environmental concerns can and do coexist with infrastructure development, but we can mitigate them by learning from experience and best practice models, both from within Africa and from other regions.[9]

The New Partnership for Africa's Development (NEPAD) has placed high priority on the need to build infrastructure, including projects on a regional basis, and end Africa's power crisis. NEPAD recently held a roundtable on Grand Inga, which attracted 120 participants from the public and private sectors, regional institutions, utility companies, nongovernmental organizations, civil society, and the media. In 2006 NEPAD launched its Infrastructure

8. See www.namtheun2.com.

9. Many of the locations that would be ideal for road or power projects in Africa are also of great importance from a conservation point of view. But detailed information is now available that can substantially mitigate the effects of new construction. A database compiled by the Global Environment Facility, the World Bank's Development Research Group, and the World Conservation Union contains information about habitats and other data relating to 5,329 amphibians, 4,612 mammals, and 1,098 endangered birds. These data enable the overlay of biodiversity maps with potential road networks to identify sensitive zones (Buys, Deichmann, and Wheeler 2006). International agencies and individual governments can tap into the scientific community's considerable expertise on biodiversity to ensure that conservation planning is a *mandatory* component of infrastructure projects in Africa.

Investment Facility (NIIF)—a private sector–led initiative to raise *domestic* financing for infrastructure projects. NEPAD is also encouraging the growing effort to raise funds for *private investment* in infrastructure. It includes six main areas—advisory services (help individual clients to bid, develop, and construct infrastructure projects), capacity building (conduct training courses, workshops, and seminars to increase the understanding of private participation in infrastructure development), clearinghouse for information (collect and disseminate information on opportunities for investment), advocacy (NIIF would advocate that governments open up infrastructure projects for private participation), collaboration (work with other technical assistance providers), and outreach (reach potential developers as well as government agencies, international institutions, and so on). NIIF is an outcome of discussions of the Africa Business Roundtable, a private sector forum that is well aware of the burden of poor roads and inadequate power supply.

There is potential to address the transport bottleneck as well, especially with strengthened regional cooperation. Buys, Deichmann, and Wheeler (2006) make a compelling argument for the creation of a major road network in sub-Saharan Africa, estimating that a network of roads connecting all sub-Saharan capitals and major cities with populations of 500,000 or more would result in an expansion of overland trade by about $250 billion over fifteen years, with both direct and indirect benefits for Africa's rural poor. They point out that overland shipments between South Africa and Nigeria—the two largest economies in Africa—are almost nonexistent because of the very poor quality of roads in transit countries such as the Democratic Republic of the Congo. Figure 4-2 presents the transnational road network proposed by Buys, Deichmann, and Wheeler along with the transcontinental corridors proposed by the African Development Bank.

Are such ambitious schemes viable? For a gain of $250 billion in trade, it does not seem difficult to justify road upgrading, even at a substantially greater cost than the $20 billion and a further $1 billion in annual maintenance estimated by Buys, Deichmann, and Wheeler. Financing mechanisms similar to those proposed above for power (for example, from OPIC) could also facilitate the development of a transnational road network on the African continent, bringing together American construction companies and African governments. Furthermore, road construction is labor intensive, and a transnational upgrading could generate much-needed jobs across several African countries.

Investments in roads should be sensitive to the need to preserve biodiversity and wildlife habitats and also include efforts to improve road safety.

Figure 4-2. A Proposed Transnational Road Network

Source: Buys, Deichmann, and Wheeler (2006).

Africa is estimated to have a very high road death rate relative to the size of its vehicle fleet—10 percent of global road deaths with only 4 percent of global vehicles (Jacobs and Aeron-Thomas 2000). This may partly reflect the fact that only 12 percent of roads in Africa are paved, but safety issues have in general received little attention or funding. As interest in infrastructure is growing and new players enter the picture, it is very important that road construction reflects safety concerns and that every available technology be considered to reduce the rate of death and injury on African roads.

Together with small-scale local power generation using new technologies, regional cooperation is therefore likely a key to easing infrastructure constraints.[10] But an active thrust toward regional cooperation requires, in the first instance, governments wanting to collaborate and, in the second, support

10. The G-8 and partners launched the Infrastructure Consortium for Africa in 2005 to ensure that financing is available for infrastructure, but funding levels (while rising) are still below the levels recommended by the Commission for Africa and the High Level Panel Report of the African

from donor institutions now structured to operate at country, rather than at regional, level. One example of successful cooperation is the West African Power Pool, in which collaborating governments have successfully given up some decisionmaking power so that the supply of electricity can be maximized on a regional basis.[11] Under the umbrella of the Economic Community of West African States (ECOWAS), heads of state meet periodically to set the terms of the regional electricity generation and distribution system. In many ways, this type of investment in large-scale infrastructure is more likely to succeed than efforts that come with less money, less international attention, and fewer safeguards.

Many donors are heavily focused on country-level programs within which incentives to encourage regional cooperation have been minimal. Several years ago, IDA (the World Bank's soft loan facility) introduced a regional project component to its funding. Energy and road projects are well suited to this new funding window, which can supply two-thirds of the funding for regional projects to complement allocations of funds from country aid envelopes. This type of funding, therefore, creates a strong incentive for national governments to cooperate. Resources for the regional component of IDA can also be used to help with grid management and with regulatory reform connected to traditional utility provision. Other donors could similarly strengthen the regional components of their programs, sending a strong signal by rewarding cooperative countries. Donor institutions can go further, however. In addition to introducing regional funds, they could also allocate part of their own operating budgets to multicountry projects on a matching basis to further provide incentives to encourage country units to collaborate on the development of regional projects.[12]

Even with improved fiscal management and aid, public funding will not be enough to plug Africa's infrastructure gap. Governments must also make

---

Development Bank (2007). At a recent meeting, the Infrastructure Consortium for Africa concluded that infrastructure needs are on the order of $38 billion per year, about two-thirds of which is required for the energy sector (ICA 2008). In 2007 consortium members committed about $10 billion in infrastructure funding. The EU-Africa Infrastructure Trust Fund, launched in 2007, is also receiving pledges from several EU member states.

11 For further information, see its website (www.ecowapp.org).

12. Regional funds from IDA hold particular promise because they can be used for projects such as the ones described above. But none of this is easy, and not just because of the scale of these projects. The World Bank Group and other aid institutions, including the African Development Bank, are largely geared to serving the national level. The World Bank, for example, is mostly organized along country units, with budgets allocated to country directors to fund work on national programs. Although this has many advantages, getting managers to work collaboratively across country

every effort to develop public-private partnerships to attract capital for the funding of infrastructure projects. Public-private partnerships (PPPs) are often mentioned as key to improving services and infrastructure in sub-Saharan Africa, where government capacity and revenue can be too limited to support the volume and size of needed investments (Farlam 2005). The opportunity to leverage private expertise and share project risk is attractive in many ways, but governments cannot expect PPPs to be the magic bullet. As with any project, corruption during tendering, implementing, and monitoring can make a viable project turn bad very quickly. And ensuring appropriate tariffs, project terms, and regulatory conditions is as essential as it is complex. Despite these difficulties, successful PPPs in sub-Saharan Africa show that they are useful instruments, provided that the project, responsibilities, and expectations are clearly defined.

African governments are fortunate that the global economy is creating large pools of savings seeking suitable investments. During a recent speech, World Bank president Robert Zoellick noted that sovereign wealth funds held an estimated $3 trillion in assets and argued that "if the World Bank Group can help create the platforms and benchmarks, the investment of even one percent of their assets would draw $30 billion to African growth, development, and opportunity" (Zoellick 2008). The World Bank and other actors can facilitate such investments in infrastructure by devising new and better instruments for underwriting and reducing risk for investments in so-called frontier markets. There is a good base to build on: The record of IDA and IBRD partial risk guarantees, discussed further below, suggests that public funding can be structured to leverage-in far greater volumes of private capital; the leverage ratio for these operations has averaged almost 10:1.

What about the maintenance of road and power projects? This is often cited as a bigger challenge than building infrastructure, but there are two reasons to be optimistic: the development of better-practice models for road construction and maintenance and the rise of a technocratic class in many African countries. Maintenance can be included in construction contracts, outsourced to independent providers, or contracted in other ways based on competitive bidding. User charges can also play a role in funding maintenance costs. Funding for

---

lines can be difficult; for staff, it means reporting to multiple country directors as well as to other managers. In sum, there are limited incentives to launch regional projects and to press for countries to collaborate. Disbursement rates on commitments to regional projects also appear low, and this may be due partly to such coordination problems and bureaucratic hurdles. While the main impetus needs to come from the countries concerned, the shareholders of aid organizations should consider how they can further reinforce internal, as well as country, incentives to cooperate.

infrastructure projects, no matter the source, must include mechanisms by which maintenance costs can be met, with these costs acknowledged upfront and provided for when the infrastructure contract is signed. One way to encourage competitive bidding is for maintenance projects to be bundled regionally, thereby providing enough scale to interest a large number of bidders.

The final potential success factor on the infrastructure front is the emerging role of China and potentially other middle-income countries such as India. Will China (and potentially India) step in to fill the infrastructure gaps in Africa? Despite the attention this question is getting, it is still quite difficult to predict how much will be achieved. China has indicated a strong interest in delivering infrastructure projects in Africa, often in exchange for natural resource concessions. Letters of intent have been signed at high-level public events; for example, in Nigeria, China has agreed to finance and build a $1.5 billion, 2,000 MW plant on the Mambila Plateau in exchange for oil exploration rights. Similar deals, involving oil or mineral resources, have been made between China and host country governments in Angola, Ethiopia, Sudan, Zambia, and Zimbabwe. Appendix 3 lists ongoing and proposed Chinese investments that reflect a strong interest in infrastructure. India also is interested in Africa's oil reserves and has entered into agreements for infrastructure development in Sudan.

The role of China in Africa is beyond the scope of this work. But it is worthwhile to take a look at what China has done in the area of infrastructure investments. Detailed data on the activities of Chinese firms have been collected by at least two organizations—the Organization for Economic Cooperation and Development (Goldstein 2007) and the Centre for Chinese Studies at Stellenbosch University in South Africa (Centre for Chinese Studies 2006). These studies shed light on countries in which China has become a major investor, including Zambia, Angola, Ethiopia, and Sierra Leone. The data show that infrastructure-related projects carried out by Chinese firms rely heavily on financing from China, that sometimes they are not competitively bid, and that they use labor from China and the host country in about equal measure. Management of the projects is, not surprisingly, carried out by the staff of the Chinese firm rather than by local staff.

At this point, we do not have sufficient information to determine what is actually happening on the ground. There are daily reports in African newspapers about new projects that will be undertaken by the Chinese government, but many of these projects have yet to take off. There is some evidence that Chinese investors are running into many of the same problems that other foreign investors encounter. Take the case of Zambia. The Zambians have made a concerted effort since 2003 to attract Chinese financing. Despite this, only one hydropower project had been completed as of 2007—the Kariba North dam. This is not to say that investment is not moving forward. In the construction sector in Ethiopia and Angola, for example, there is a large and visible Chinese presence. But in Angola, which has been a main target of Chinese interest, given its oil reserves, less has happened than was previously anticipated. Some fairly large-scale road construction projects have begun, but recently the *Financial Times* reports that several projects have been stalled, downsized, or simply never started. China has run into some of the same problems that other countries and donor agencies have encountered, such as unforeseen delays and cost overruns. Recently, the Angolan government revised estimates of its lines of credit from China downward by two-thirds.[13]

In the medium-to-long run, China, and potentially other middle-income countries, probably will make a considerable contribution to the enormous task of infrastructure building. At present, its companies are certainly providing stiff competition for the traditional contractors for infrastructure, something that is potentially to Africa's advantage. But for now, one should be patient in assessing China's performance in Africa. The popular fear about China and its motives in Africa vastly exceeds knowledge of actual events.

Regional Integration: Wider Markets, Increased Economic Density, and Greater Competition

Infrastructure is not the only argument in favor of regional or pan-African economic ties. The surveys suggest that in terms of opening up space for greater competition, and also potentially for increasing economic density, regional integration of markets in Africa can play a significant role.

Regional integration of markets and the accompanying harmonization of customs, regulations, and trading rules will expand the size of the market and the number of firms in the marketplace. This will reduce firms' market shares from their currently very high levels, making it harder and less worthwhile for any given domestically entrenched enterprise to invest resources to retain market share. Regional integration might also meet with less resistance as opposed to further trade liberalization if local firms perceive that additional profits may be made in a larger regional market.

13. Alec Russell, "Infrastructure: Big Projects Fall behind Schedule," *Financial Times*, January 24, 2008, p. 3.

An expanded regional market that is not dominated by any single government or firm and in which the gains from entry are potentially larger relative to the costs of establishment may also make it easier for new firms to enter the picture. This will impact economic density as well as increase levels of competition. To the extent that they present a new opportunity to increase the size of the market while attracting new entrants, regional reforms may be easier to implement than some other types of reforms.

Regional integration could also spur greater competition for investment, not only between national governments but among subnational governments. In much of East Asia, competition has been a hallmark of development, not only among firms but also among national and local governments vying for investment and seeking to overtake competing jurisdictions. In China, for example, from the early years of reform onward, communities have competed vigorously with each other for investors and resources (Byrd and Gelb 1990). States and regions continue to benchmark their performance against each other and compete.[14] States in India are now also beginning to compete for investment and new business.

How can such competition be unleashed in Africa, where most jurisdictions have a low density of economic activity? In addition to the opening of regional markets, which will help to establish a wider range of benchmarks, fiscal arrangements might be reviewed to encourage active competition—at present, in contrast to China, they provide limited incentive to municipalities to compete. This could include introducing municipal incentive funds that are based on a municipality's success in attracting investors, as well as competitions offering prizes and free publicity to successful municipalities. Performance-based incentives could also be considered for key providers of business services, such as port management and customs and tax administration. These would need to be based on a combination of fiscal revenue targets (when appropriate) and business-related performance indicators, such as clearance or transit time. None of this will happen, however, unless national governments themselves are convinced of the need to become regionally or globally competitive.

Broadening the Base of the Private Sector

In his seminal work on Africa published over two decades ago, Robert Bates provided several reasons for why governments were slow to pursue market-

---

14. For the example of Singapore and Johore province in Malaysia, see Kassim (2006).

based reforms (Bates 1981). Despite decades of donor advice and some significant reforms, it is still relatively difficult to find policymakers who really trust markets to deliver results; given the choice, governments often prefer a regulatory or administrative solution (Emery 2003). Governments are sometimes concerned that liberalizations or reforms will benefit already entrenched business groups. In other cases, of course, they may be concerned that reforms are potentially threatening to the position of the relatively few large businesses, which often have large market shares and long-standing relationships with governments.

How can governments be convinced that a broad-based, relatively unfettered private sector is both possible and in their interest? As noted above, some governments have tried drastic measures to curb the rights of minority entrepreneurs, but these have not resulted in viable opportunities for indigenous entrepreneurs. Others fear the emergence of a private sector that will be "unmanageable," but experience from around the world suggests that a more competitive private sector will not immediately translate into a threat to whoever is in office. Available evidence shows that for the most part, reforms to promote private sector development have led, at least in the early stages, to a proliferation of small and medium-size firms in countries such as Taiwan and Malaysia. These firms are hardly a challenge to political incumbents and indeed are probably less likely to lead to political problems than systems that foster the rise of a small, wealthy class of tycoons and the continued dominance of a minority ethnic group.

A first point to emphasize is that reforms that benefit a large number of firms, such as licensing reforms, the abolition of "nuisance taxes" and regulations that serve only to make firms more vulnerable to harassment, and improvement of the functioning of financial markets (including setting up credit and asset registries, which seem to be potentially important in widening the access to finance), should be pursued as energetically as those focusing on trade, which may be seen as benefiting importers and larger exporting firms more than anyone else. Benchmarking regulatory performance in these areas can be helpful. Tax regimes, too, need to be reviewed to ensure equity.

Strong links can be created between institutions carrying out systematic research on the business climate and public-private consultative groups tasked with recommending approaches to reforms and contributing to the design of reforms. This can help to ensure a substantive agenda of reform that is underpinned by sound analysis.

The "network effect" within minority ethnic groups may be of particular significance in Africa, as information flows and contract enforceability are weak in much of the region. Minority entrepreneurs within a network have greater incentive to stick to their contractual obligations since members of the network will monitor contracts and inflict penalties for violations. Indigenous entrepreneurs who are not operating within a network are not bound by these types of enforcement mechanisms, nor are they able to generate enough credible information to enable them to access trade credit and other resources. Members of the network have detailed knowledge of each other's firms and the characteristics of the owners and managers; this enables a positive flow of credit, technology, and other resources on terms that are unavailable to firms outside the network.

In these conditions there may be a concern that the real beneficiaries of reforms will be a small group of entrenched firms, often composed of ethnic minorities. Some populist governments have in the past sought to penalize ethnic minority groups to promote indigenous entrepreneurs, but the undermining of confidence in the business sector has made such efforts very costly and counterproductive. Efforts are therefore needed to help indigenous businesses and create alternative, competing networks. These concerns can be addressed with interventions that will help small domestic investors operate sustainable businesses.

One essential component will be higher education. The surveys show that university education is significant in determining the performance and rate of growth of indigenous businesses. This result may partly reflect the role of education in easing entry into a network of business professionals that serves as an alternative to ethnic minority networks. Access to a network may enable the flow of information—about business performance, characteristics of the entrepreneur, and other vital data that enable lending, the supply of trade credit, and the transfer of technological know-how. If this is the case, it points to the need for more and better education, whether it comes through formal educational institutions or some other type of training directly related to business-specific skills. It might also be in the form of workshops or entrepreneurial boot camps. Enhancing local capacity to provide such training should be an important objective. Outside of South Africa, African business schools are generally much in need of skills enhancement and curriculum development. Initiatives such as the Global Business School Network (GBSN) that seek to build the capacity of selected African business schools by bringing them together with leading business schools in industrial countries can play a role. Until recently, for example, there were no African business cases to provide teaching materials; under the auspices of the GBSN, case writers have been trained and sets of Anglophone and Francophone cases have now been produced and are in active use in East and West Africa.[15]

Is there scope for affirmative action in the African context? Countries such as South Africa and Zambia have launched major initiatives, such as the Black Empowerment Act, to address the huge gaps between the indigenous and non-indigenous populations. Several other countries, including Liberia, are considering legislation that would grant certain groups preferential access to loans, equity, and services. But is this a good idea? A detailed discussion of affirmative action is beyond the scope of this book. But it is worth noting a recent paper from the Brenthurst Foundation in South Africa. It discussed Malaysia's efforts in this area and concluded that affirmative action may have some relevance, if implemented according to strict guidelines (Stead 2007). The Malaysian program stressed participation in, rather than control over, the economy by the indigenous population, thereby making its programs more viable. But in the end, it has not increased participation by all that much. Malay ownership in the local economy stood at 18.4 percent in 1990 in contrast to the goal of 30 percent. Steve Stead argues that there should be a clear time limit on such programs and that they often "run the risk of becoming divisive and self-defeating." Writing in the context of South Africa, he concludes that securing commitment of the nonindigenous population to the future is at least as important as attempts to increase local ownership. Capital flight at the first sign of trouble is suggested to be perhaps the most damaging aspect of the current ownership pattern in South Africa and elsewhere.

Another option to encourage domestic investors could be to make available more broadly some of the programs that have been used to encourage foreign investment. Partial risk guarantees from the World Bank and IDA have been used for the last decade to facilitate private investment in large infrastructure projects. Experience from twenty-eight projects around the world suggests that leverage ratios are quite high, with total guarantees of $2.9 billion catalyzing private capital of almost $30 billion, for an average leverage ratio of close to 10:1. Examples in Africa include Azito Power and the West Africa Gas Pipeline.[16] In such operations, aid can be used to enhance

15. For more information on business school development in Africa, the reader is directed to the Management Education & Research Consortium, which works in partnership with members of the Global Business School Network and the Association of African Business Schools. See its website (www.mercnetwork.org/).

16. The Multilateral Investment Guarantee Agency's Africa portfolio has also been growing rapidly. Twenty-one contracts totaling $180 million were concluded in 2006, many in traded goods sectors such as agribusiness, manufacturing, and tourism. Programs have also been initiated to use guarantees to

credit quality by providing a "first loss" reserve that enables private insurers to provide cover at lower cost.

An essential step in leveling the playing field would be to offer partial risk guarantees to *domestic* investors on an equal basis with external investors, including long-term savers like pension and insurance funds. Except possibly for the repatriation of investment and profits, most of the contingencies covered by a partial risk guarantee, such as expropriation and government failure to fulfill contractual obligations, apply equally to domestic and foreign investors. That would require developing an appropriate process to deal with covered domestic investments, a step that would not seem to be insuperable. For example, domestic pension and insurance funds might be covered through the syndication of their financing with that of covered external investors. Wider application would likely require specific arrangements with governments on the treatment of covered domestic investors.

Partial risk guarantees could also be broadened to include "service guarantees," which also would be available to domestic and foreign investors on an equal basis. Under such an approach, countries implementing reforms in key areas such as power, customs, licensing, and so on, would commit themselves to service standards. Firms could purchase insurance against service failures, perhaps not on an individual basis (since that would invite moral hazard) but on the basis of overall performance. These contracts would be underwritten by risk guarantee programs, possibly funded by donor countries through international financial institution (IFI) programs. Widespread or persistent failure to provide business services to agreed standards would then activate the guarantee. This would do more than just compensate firms for lost business. It would force the question of business service standards to become a priority topic of discussion among policymakers. The guarantees would then serve two purposes: to provide risk mitigation for investors and to strengthen the credibility of reforms in the business environment and of performance-based government.

How might such guarantees work? Although they are a form of insurance, service guarantees could not be implemented like political risk guarantees: the transaction costs of such an approach would be prohibitive because they would cover large numbers of businesses, providing relatively small payments against periodic service lapses. Using available data, governments and firms would need to reach a consensus on the most serious impediments to investment and the effective operation of existing businesses. These might include

---

increase the volume of trade credit, an area of particular interest for smaller firms not able to tap into existing networks.

the unreliability of power supply, slow port and customs clearance times for imported inputs and for exports, long delays in rebating import duties or VAT to exporters, and poor security.

Donors may already have projects that address these areas. A private sector program, encompassing all of these projects, would aim for an agreed set of performance standards, between the private sector and the government, and systems for monitoring performance. Some services can be benchmarked against international norms. Businesses, perhaps starting with those in export processing zones (EPZs), would be offered the opportunity to purchase service guarantees. The guarantee would not insure against lapses in service provided to that particular business; it would insure against lapses in average service provided to firms in general (perhaps starting with those in EPZs). This is necessary to avoid moral hazard and also to simplify monitoring.

To ensure that firms would not be able to profit just by betting on the performance of government, payouts would be subject to two ceilings, one related to the level of insurance purchased by a firm and the other to the volume of sales or exports. Monitoring would be on a monthly basis; it would be part of the performance agreement between government and the responsible ministry underpinning the private sector program; and it would be reviewed by a tripartite commission representing government, the private sector, and the funding donors. Lapses in performance beyond specified levels would trigger automatic compensatory payments to covered businesses. For firms in an EPZ, for example, these could be provided simply in the form of rebates on rent, fees, and other service charges. In cases of extreme nonperformance, fees inclusive of rebates would be negative. Only in truly extreme cases (for example, war or severe natural disasters) would the service standards be waived.

Compensatory payments above the levels of funding provided by the premiums would be provided from a fund guaranteed by donors through a component of the private sector operation. Total liability would be capped at a multiple of the total payments by firms that would be accepted in a given operation (for example, total liability of up to ten times the premiums) and a limit set on the term of the guarantee program (about ten years). Calls on the guarantee facility would trigger a government counterguarantee to the donor (for example, if to World Bank, this would be funded by an IDA credit that would come out of the country allocation).

This type of program could offer several potential benefits to the private sector. By forcing governments, businesses, and donors to focus on service delivery results, it would provide a framework for capacity building and investment. Without picking winners, it could play a role in encouraging investment, especially in export-oriented activities, and could serve as an important signal to potential investors that the private sector is taken seriously by the government. Most important, it would enhance the level of policy dialogue and reform in the business environment area by restructuring accountability, ensuring that governments and development partners bear some real accountability for poor implementation of programs in this area. Even if firms do not sign up for the program in large numbers, many of its purposes are served—with performance shortfalls, small guarantee payments are made, performance lapses are documented, and the issue is pushed to high levels of policy dialogue.

Conclusion

Africa's infrastructure needs pose an enormous and urgent challenge. Rather than focus on conventional, national-level investments in power and roads, we argue that large-scale investments made under regional cooperation agreements will yield the greatest benefits. Africa's vast potential for renewable energy sources suggests another avenue as well—very small-scale technology to harness solar and hydropower that will power villages and small towns without having to rely on a public grid. Finally, a transcontinental road network has the potential to increase overland trade within the continent itself.

The base of the private sector remains very small and must be broadened to sustain a vibrant business sector and a middle class. To achieve this, we propose that commonalities of purpose be identified and be used as the basis for merging the various business forums that currently exist in any given country. The business-government dialogue can be strengthened by such convergence, and real gains can be made against the constraints faced by the private sector. Investments in education, especially to build entrepreneurial skills, are also important to build a broad-based private sector.

Finally, rich countries must support the efforts of individuals and governments, *but they must also do no harm.*[17] Large amounts of aid can lower the need for private sector reforms because they can be seen as replacements for tax revenues that would otherwise be generated from the private sector. In the longer term, dependence on donors can lead to real disincentives to reform and grow. Rich countries need to balance this problem with the need to provide financing in critical areas such as infrastructure and training.

17. Birdsall (2007).

Appendixes

Appendix 1. Regression Results

Table A-1. Determinants of Total Factor Productivity

Variable	Low income			Middle income			Lower middle income		
Intercept	5.72*** (0.248)	5.91*** (0.269)	5.72*** (0.246)	7.29*** (0.215)	7.31*** (0.216)	7.21*** (0.217)	5.90*** (0.236)	5.97*** (0.237)	6.03*** (0.243)
Log(capital)	0.24*** (0.017)	0.24*** (0.017)	0.22*** (0.018)	0.21*** (0.019)	0.21*** (0.019)	0.21*** (0.019)	0.30*** (0.022)	0.30*** (0.022)	0.29*** (0.023)
Log(labor)	0.71*** (0.042)	0.71*** (0.042)	0.69*** (0.042)	0.83*** (0.034)	0.83*** (0.034)	0.81*** (0.035)	0.63*** (0.043)	0.63*** (0.042)	0.62*** (0.043)
Food	-0.05 (0.094)	-0.06 (0.094)	-0.06 (0.093)	-0.22** (0.100)	-0.20** (0.101)	-0.21** (0.100)	-0.12 (0.102)	-0.13 (0.103)	-0.13 (0.102)
Textile and garment	-0.39 (0.118)	-0.37 (0.119)	-0.35*** (0.118)	-0.55*** (0.101)	-0.55*** (0.101)	-0.51*** (0.102)	-0.23* (0.116)	-0.25** (0.117)	-0.21* (0.116)
Wood and furniture	-0.17 (0.101)	-0.17 (0.103)	-0.12 (0.101)	-0.17 (0.103)	-0.06 (0.103)	-0.18* (0.103)	0.08 (0.132)	0.06 (0.132)	0.12 (0.132)
Metal	-0.06 (0.120)	-0.04 (0.122)	-0.03 (0.119)	-0.16 (0.102)	-0.17* (0.102)	-0.16 (0.102)	0.13 (0.137)	0.11 (0.137)	0.13 (0.136)
Chemical	0.25 (0.154)	0.24 (0.155)	0.22 (0.153)	0.08 (0.119)	0.08 (0.119)	0.09 (0.119)	-0.05 (0.187)	-0.07 (0.187)	-0.03 (0.188)
Export	0.09 (0.120)	0.09 (0.107)	0.10 (0.105)	-0.07 (0.084)	-0.07 (0.084)	-0.07 (0.085)	0.15 (0.104)	0.14 (0.104)	0.13 (0.104)
Foreign owned	0.18** (0.091)	0.18** (0.092)	0.14 (0.091)	0.26*** (0.085)	0.25*** (0.085)	0.26*** (0.085)	0.16 (0.110)	0.16 (0.110)	0.13 (0.104)
Sales lost due to outages	-0.04 (0.301)	—	—	-0.11 (1.370)	—	—	-1.33** (0.533)	—	—
Transport losses	1.01** (0.502)	—	—	-1.13* (0.628)	—	—	-0.32 (0.490)	—	—
Own generator	—	—	0.33*** (0.077)	—	—	0.14* (0.083)	—	—	0.21*** (0.092)
Own transportation	—	—	0.09 (0.079)	—	—	0.10 (0.067)	—	—	0.01 (0.079)
ISO certification	0.78*** (0.105)	0.79*** (0.107)	0.74*** (0.105)	0.39*** (0.078)	0.40*** (0.078)	0.39*** (0.078)	0.29*** (0.119)	0.30*** (0.119)	0.28*** (0.119)

	(1)	(2)	(3)	(4)	(5)	(6)	(7)	(8)	(9)
Train	(0.060) (0.076)	0.05 (0.077)	0.07 (0.075)	0.12* (0.069)	0.11 (0.069)	0.13* (0.069)	0.11 (0.085)	0.14 (0.086)	0.10 (0.085)
Website	0.43*** (0.114)	0.44*** (0.115)	0.38*** (0.114)	0.25*** (0.077)	0.25*** (0.077)	0.24*** (0.077)	0.15 (0.109)	0.15 (0.109)	0.11 (0.110)
Burundi	0.39* (0.216)	0.24 (0.241)	0.47** (0.215)						
DR Congo	0.59*** (0.206)	0.44* (0.232)	0.69*** (0.206)						
Uganda	0.35* (0.196)	0.19 (0.223)	0.51*** (0.197)						
Tanzania	0.98*** (0.198)	0.79*** (0.224)	1.06*** (0.197)						
Rwanda	0.46* (0.237)	0.31 (0.260)	0.56*** (0.237)						
Guinea	0.72*** (0.212)	0.54*** (0.238)	0.69*** (0.211)						
Guinea-Bissau	(0.210) (0.239)	0.04 (0.263)	0.18 (0.237)						
Namibia				0.24 (0.160)	0.24 (0.160)	0.25 (0.160)			
South Africa				0.35*** (0.132)	0.35*** (0.132)	0.37*** (0.132)			
Botswana				-0.21 (0.154)	-0.21 (0.155)	-0.21 (0.156)			
Kenya							0.64*** (0.121)	0.67*** (0.122)	0.60*** (0.122)
Angola							0.58*** (0.127)	0.61*** (0.127)	0.46*** (0.139)
N	954	939	954	915	915	915	640	638	640
Adjusted R squared	0.7473	0.7471	0.7525	0.7578	0.7582	0.7588	0.7589	0.7606	0.7602

Source: Authors' calculations.

***Significant at the 1 percent level; **significant at the 5 percent level; *significant at the 10 percent level.

DR Congo = Democratic Republic of the Congo; ISO = International Organization for Standardization.

— Not applicable.

Table A-2. Probit Estimations of Access to Credit

	All businesses			Indigenous		
	Current loan	Overdraft	Trade credit	Current loan	Overdraft	Trade credit
Intercept	−1.41*** (0.211)	−1.28*** (0.216)	0.08 (0.204)	−0.94*** (0.246)	−1.70*** (0.263)	−0.24 (0.230)
Log(workers)	0.32*** (0.034)	0.34*** (0.035)	0.16*** (0.033)	0.31*** (0.050)	0.39*** (0.053)	0.17*** (0.046)
Log(firm age)	−0.07 (0.049)	0.03 (0.051)	0.05 (0.045)	−0.05 (0.066)	0.02 (0.069)	0.07 (0.056)
University education	0.07 (0.078)	0.21** (0.082)	0.04 (0.072)	−0.01 (0.099)	0.27** (0.105)	0.07 (0.086)
Indigenous	−0.23*** (0.085)	−0.21** (0.085)	−0.23*** (0.080)	—	—	—
Own land	0.42*** (0.074)	0.30*** (0.078)	0.05 (0.069)	0.40*** (0.098)	0.22** (0.105)	0.08 (0.084)
Burundi	0.17 (0.186)	−0.20 (0.193)	−1.17*** (0.193)	−0.14 (0.221)	−0.30 (0.235)	−1.18*** (0.229)
DR Congo	−1.11*** (0.200)	−1.50*** (0.221)	−1.20*** (0.173)	−1.48*** (0.272)	−1.74*** (0.350)	−1.03*** (0.212)
Uganda	−0.70*** (0.156)	−1.06*** (0.164)	−0.61*** (0.151)	−0.91*** (0.192)	−1.16*** (0.210)	−0.57** (0.182)
Angola	−1.65*** (0.220)	−1.97*** (0.277)	−1.45*** (0.174)	−2.08*** (0.287)	−2.01*** (0.344)	−1.48*** (0.205)
Swaziland	−0.56*** (0.207)	−0.19 (0.207)	0.19 (0.217)	−0.55** (0.262)	−0.30 (0.274)	0.16 (0.270)
Namibia	−0.11 (0.181)	0.43** (0.181)	0.29 (0.190)	−0.13 (0.225)	0.59*** (0.230)	0.27 (0.231)
Rwanda	0.19 (0.218)	−0.32 (0.219)	−1.20*** (0.222)	0.21 (0.262)	−0.24 (0.263)	−1.14*** (0.265)
Tanzania	−0.57*** (0.155)	−0.84*** (0.160)	−0.70*** (0.152)	−0.81*** (0.197)	−0.81*** (0.208)	−0.76*** (0.189)
Kenya	0.24 (0.144)	0.06 (0.148)	0.17 (0.151)	0.18 (0.196)	0.04 (0.205)	0.22 (0.200)
The Gambia	−0.42 (0.283)	0.07 (0.271)	−0.87*** (0.267)	−0.54* (0.312)	0.23 (0.301)	−0.75*** (0.293)
Guinea	−1.08*** (0.225)	−0.80*** (0.210)	−1.01*** (0.180)	−1.62*** (0.297)	−0.88*** (0.250)	−0.96*** (0.208)
Mauritania	−0.43** (0.203)	−0.47** (0.206)	−0.35* (0.194)	−0.58** (0.232)	−0.43* (0.240)	−0.27 (0.221)
Food	−0.05 (0.091)	−0.07 (0.095)	−0.07 (0.086)	−0.01 (0.122)	0.08 (0.130)	−0.03 (0.108)
Textiles and garments	−0.37*** (0.110)	−0.39** (0.114)	−0.41*** (0.104)	−0.26* (0.151)	−0.02 (0.161)	−0.42 (0.134)
Wood and furniture	−0.26** (0.110)	−0.18 (0.115)	−0.14 (0.097)	−0.32** (0.136)	−0.03 (0.145)	−0.15 (0.115)
Metal	0.01 (0.122)	−0.02 (0.129)	−0.05 (0.113)	−0.15 (0.165)	−0.09 (0.178)	−0.17 (0.137)

(continued)

Table A-2. Probit Estimations of Access to Credit (continued)

	All businesses			Indigenous		
	Current loan	Overdraft	Trade credit	Current loan	Overdraft	Trade credit
Log likelihood	−907.5	−819.57	−1100.5	−537.21	−465.72	−767.28
N	2,026	2,026	2,022	1,395	1,395	1,395

Source: Authors' calculations.
***Significant at the 1 percent level; **significant at the 5 percent level; *significant at the 10 percent level.
DR Congo = Democratic Republic of the Congo.
— Not applicable.

Table A-3. Econometric Estimations of Growth

	Growth rate			Size at start		
Variable	All businesses	Indigenous	Minority	All businesses	Indigenous	Minority
Intercept	0.26*** −0.012	0.245*** −0.014	0.272*** −0.03	2.097*** −0.146	1.668*** −0.137	2.481*** −0.423
Log(employment at start)	−0.034*** −0.002	−0.004*** −0.003	−0.024*** −0.003			
Log(firm age)	−0.050*** −0.002	−0.042*** −0.003	0.062*** −0.005			
Log(years of experience)				0.059** −0.027	0.101*** −0.029	−0.025 −0.061
Foreign ownership	0.015*** −0.005	0.020*** −0.009	0.008 −0.008	0.178*** −0.065	0.208*** −0.093	0.191* −0.11
Secondary education	−0.011 −0.007	−0.006 −0.007	−0.032 −0.026	0.013 −0.081	0.068 −0.075	−0.632 −0.373
Vocational education	−0.001 −0.006	0.001 −0.007	0.6416 −0.025	0.041 −0.078	0.105 −0.073	−0.584 −0.366
University education	0.011* −0.006	0.013* −0.007	−0.002 −0.024	0.476*** −0.076	0.441*** −0.072	−0.009 −0.349
Postgraduate degree	0.018*** −0.008	0.022*** −0.01	0.001 −0.024	0.856*** −0.091	0.854*** −0.101	0.391 −0.355
Overdraft	0.03*** −0.005	0.031*** −0.006	0.029*** −0.007	0.461*** −0.056	0.408*** −0.065	0.503*** −0.104
Indigenous	−0.021*** −0.005			−0.555*** −0.062		
Food	0 −0.005	−0.004 −0.006	0.004 −0.008	0.212*** −0.059	0.185*** −0.065	0.217* −0.12
Textile and garments	−0.001 −0.006	−0.012* −0.007	0.003 −0.01	0.054 −0.069	−0.265*** −0.076	0.661*** −0.146
Wood and furniture	−0.006 −0.005	−0.01 −0.006	0 −0.013	−0.027 −0.066	−0.105 −0.068	−0.104 −0.186
Metal working	−0.004 −0.006	−0.009 −0.008	0.003 −0.012	0.003 −0.078	−0.116 −0.083	0.165 −0.181
N	2,025	1,417	601	2,029	1,420	602
Adjusted R squared	0.3317	0.3508	0.3307	0.2964	0.2247	0.1681

Source: Authors' calculations.
***Significant at the 1 percent level; **significant at the 5 percent level; *significant at the 10 percent level.

Appendix 2. Venture Capital–Funded Solar Energy Projects

Firm	Location	Contribution to solar market	Investors (or past investors)
United States			
Advent Solar	Albuquerque, N. Mex.	Thin-film wafers that use less silicon; simplified assembly, higher energy production to drive down costs; locates all electrical content on back of solar cell to free up top surface for more sunlight absorption	ZBI Ventures; Sun Mountain Capital; Globespan Capital Partners; Battery Ventures; EnerTech; Firelank Capital; @Ventures; New Mexico Co-Investment Partners
Akeena Solar	Los Gatos, Calif.	Provider of solar energy systems	Kleiner Perkins Caufield & Byers
Ausra	Palo Alto, Calif.	Designing solar-thermal power plants to be deployed in the desert	Kleiner Perkins Caufield & Byers; Khosla Ventures
BrightSource Energy	Oakland, Calif.	Utility-scale solar thermal power plant that uses mirrors to focus solar rays on water to convert it to steam and drive turbines	VantagePoint Venture Partners
Energy Innovation	Pasadena, Calif.	Solar chip manufacturer; Sunflower product tracks sunbeams and produces both PV power and hot water	Mohr, Davidow Ventures; Idealab Holdings LLC
HelioVolt	Austin, Tex.	Uses CIGS technology; claims it can achieve efficiencies near those of silicon cells but with 1/100 of the material; reusable template capable of mass producing material	Paladin Capital Group; Masdar Clean Tech Fund; New Enterprise Associates; Solucar Energias; Morgan Stanley Principal Investments; Sunton United Energy; Yellowstone Capital
INFINIA Corp.	Kennewick, Wash.	High-efficiency heat and power systems; solar generators	Khosla Ventures; Vulcan Capital; EQUUS Total Return, Inc; Idealab; Power Play Energy, LLC
Innovalight Inc.	Santa Clara, Calif.	Low-cost panels; new technology for printing solar material onto a substrate	Harris & Harris Group Inc.; Apax Partners; Arch Venture Partners; Sevin Rosen Funds; Triton Ventures
Konarka	Lowell, Mass.	Leading in the arena of organic solar cells; technology relies on a dye to absorb solar energy; could be incorporated into flexible panels or fabrics	Draper Fisher Jurvetson; ChevronTexaco; New Enterprise Associates
Luz II	Oakland, Calif.	Low-cost panels; flat glass in mirrors that track the sun as it moves; solar thermal	VantagePoint Venture Partners

Company	Location	Description	Investors/Partners
Miasole	San Jose, Calif.	Makes thin-film solar cells with less semiconductor material than traditional silicon-based cells (less than 1 percent of the silicon of traditional cells); designing a continuous manufacturing process (more and faster automation) that should help reduce costs; pursuing CIGS technology that is higher efficiency	VantagePoint Venture Partners; Kleiner Perkins Caulfield & Byers
MWOE	Toledo, Ohio	Pilot production line to demonstrate its high-volume, low-cost method of making solar cells on a stainless steel substrate no thicker than a sheet of paper.	Emerald Technology Ventures; NPG Energy Technology Partners
Nanosolar	Palo Alto, Calif.	Thin-film solar panels and continuous manufacturing process to reduce costs; copper thin-film panels will cost 5–10x less than silicon panels; pursuing CIGS technology and is looking at solutions to efficiency-loss of CIGS over large areas; designing cells to be more flexible and attractive than other solar panels, perhaps included in building materials; boss projects company will achieve grid parity this year; building world's largest solar cell fabrication lab near San Francisco; building panel fabrication facility in Berlin	Larry Page & Sergey Brin; Mohr, Davidow Ventures; US Venture Partners; OnPoint Technologies; Benchmark Capital; Capricorn Management LLC; SAC Capital Advisors LLC; GLG Partners LP; Grazia Equity GmbH; Beck Energy GmbH; Klaus Tschira; Dietmar Hopp; Christian Reitberger; Jeff Skoll
Petra Solar	Green Brook, N.J.	Creating portfolio of semiconductor patents and a variety of products to boost efficiency and power management capabilities of solar power	DFJ Element; Blue Run Ventures; National Technology Enterprises Co.
Practical Instruments Inc.	Pasadena, Calif.	Uses optical technology to try to reduce the cost of rooftop solar panels; uses less PV material per panel	Nth Power; RockPort Capital Partners; Trinity Ventures; Rincon Venture Partners
Silicon Valley Solar Inc.	Santa Clara, Calif.	Acquired NuEdison Inc., a maker of PV modules; designs modules that concentrate energy in flat panels; uses an advanced internal concentrator; sells to large solar integrators	Bessemer Venture Partners

(continued)

Appendix 2. Venture Capital–Funded Solar Energy Projects (continued)

Firm	Location	Contribution to solar market	Investors (or past investors)
Solaicx	Santa Clara, Calif.	Dedicated to cutting costs of single crystalline wafers for the solar industry; aims to cut 75 percent of cost of solar cell manufacturing	Applied Materials; DE Shaw Group; Mitsui Ventures; Applied Ventures LLC; Firsthand Capital Management Inc.; Big Sky Ventures; Greenhouse Capital Partners
Solar Notion	Sunnyvale, Calif.	Developing low-cost technology; improving efficiency and reliability of single crystal silicon panels	Third Point
Solaria	Fremont, Calif.	Developing process to make solar panels more efficient and cheaper to manufacture	Sigma Partners; NGEN
SolFocus	Palo Alto, Calif.	Uses lenses and mirrors to concentrate sunlight onto high-efficiency solar cells to reduce cost per watt; increases efficiency of cells	New Enterprise Associates; NGEN
SoloPower Inc.	Milpitas, Calif.	CIGS technology thin-film manufacturer; can be made in large batches that can help reduce costs	Convexa Capital; Scatec AS; Spencer Energy AS; Crosslink Capital; Firsthand Capital Management
Stion Corp (formerly nStructures)	Menlo Park, Calif.	Developing thin-films that lower the cost of manufacturing models; improving efficiency of crystalline silicon materials	Lightspeed Venture Partners; General Catalyst Partners; Khosla Ventures; Braemar Energy Ventures; Moser Baer Photovoltaic
Stirling Energy Systems	Phoenix, Ariz.	Goal to build world's largest solar facility using panels with concentrating technology	
Tioga Energy Inc.	San Mateo, Calif.	Provides solar systems to customers; guarantees predictable costs	NGEN; Draper Fisher Jurvetson; RockPort Capital; DFJ Frontier; Kirlan Ventures
Envision Solar	San Diego, Calif.	Turns parking lots into solar farms	

Non–United States

Company	Location	Description	Investors
6N Silicon Inc.	Mississauga, Ontario, Canada	Produces solar-grade silicon tailored specifically for the solar industry	Ventures West; Yaletown Venture Partners
Bright Light Solar	Wales, U.K.	Provides remote, off-grid electricity solutions	Apax Partners; Good Energies Inc.; Renewable Energy Corp.; IBG Beteiligungsgesellschaft Sachsen-Anhalt mbH
CSG Solar AG	Thalheim, Germany	Manufactures thin-film on glass modules that uses less silicon and has fewer production steps	
Day4 Energy	Vancouver, British Columbia, Canada	Produces flat-panel modules with an electrode that reduces the resistance of a traditional PV cell; produces sun concentrators	Chrysalix Energy; British Columbia Discovery Fund
EnerWorks	London, Ontario, Canada	Manufactures solar thermal products, including solar power water heaters; goal of reducing water heating energy costs	Chrysalix Energy; Investeco Capital
G24 Innovations (G24i)	Cardiff, Wales, U.K.	Non-silicon-based cells; cells based on colored dye and titantium oxide crystals that are used to copy photosynthesis; estimated at 1/5 price of silicon cells; working with mobile phone companies to test whether cells could be used to charge handsets in rural Africa; plan to sell inexpensive devices (for lightbulb or cell phone charging) in poor regions of India and Africa to jumpstart sales	Renewable Capital
Hydrogen Solar	United Kingdom	Uses sunlight to generate hydrogen fuel	E-Synergy
Jiamgsu Shunda Group	China	Makes 6-inch and 8-inch monocrystalline silicon ingots used in solar power cells	Actis; JOLMO Capital Management; Waichun
Orionsolar	Jerusalem, Israel	Uses dye cell nanotechnology that does not use silicon; trying to build a low-cost energy panel	21 Ventures LLC
Solarcentury Holdings Ltd.	London	Designs and installs solar modules	VantagePoint Venture Partners
Solel	Beit Shemesh, Israel	Parabolic solar trough technology used for solar thermal electricity	

Source: Authors' compilation.

Appendix 3. A Partial Listing of China's Investment in Africa

Country	Amount (dollars)	Date	Project	Terms and conditions	Financier
Angola	211 million	Announced August 2005	Road rehabilitation		Exim Bank
Angola	2 billion in 2004, risen to 6 billion by 2007	2004–07	Hospitals, schools; roads, bridges, housing, office buildings, training programs, laying of fiber-optic cable		
Angola	3 billion	Signed March 2006	Oil refinery		
Angola	300 million	2006	Rehabilitate Benguela railroad		ZTE Corp.
Angola	300 million	2005	Modernize communications network		ZTE Corp.
Angola	69 million	2005	Develop telephone networks		ZTE Corp.
Angola	100 million	2005	Military communications, mobile phone factory, telecom training institute		
Botswana	17 million	Signed summer 2006	Construction of Lethakeng Kang road		
Cameroon	47 million	Pledged in January 2007	Telecom project	Concessional loan	
DR Congo	8.5 billion	September 2007	Road, rail construction	Rights to copper and cobalt reserves	
DR Congo	5 billion	Announced September 2007	Road and rail construction projects; rehabilitation of mining sector	Repayment terms include mining concessions and toll revenue deals	
DR Congo	5 billion	November 2007	Joint mining venture with Gecamines in return for loans for infrastructure	68 percent of joint venture; mineral rights	
DR Congo	9 billion	April 2008	$3 billion to reopen a copper and cobalt mine, $6 billion on roads, rail, hospitals, universities	10 million tons of copper; 400,000 tons of cobalt	Exim Bank

Country	Amount	Date	Project	Terms	Lender
DR Congo	2.9 billion	April 2008	Infrastructure development for mining venture	10 million tons of copper and cobalt; concessional loans ($500 million at 0 percent interest)	China Railway Group
Djibouti	12 million	Signed July 2003	Rehabilitation of telecom infrastructure	Three-year grace period; concessional rate of 2 percent per year	Exim Bank
Ethiopia			Tekeze hydro dam		
Ethiopia	200 million (reports of up to 1.5 billion)	Signed April 2007	Three telecom expansion projects including first phase of fiber transmission backbone		
Gabon	Several billion dollars	Announced March 2007	Extractive infrastructure at Belinga iron mine; hydroelectric dam; railway to coast; deepwater port north of Libreville	Won contract to develop the Belinga iron ore deposit	
Ghana	28 million	Completed June 2006	Upgraded highway from Accra to Ghana's second largest city	Interest-free loan	
Ghana	108 million	Signed June 2006	Part of the loan goes toward national telecom backbone; expansion of mobile and fixed networks	Largely concessionary	
Ghana	622 million	Announced summer 2007	Construction of Bui hydroelectric dam	Hybrid concessional loan and buyers credit facility	Exim Bank, partially
Kenya	28 million	Agreement in April	Various development projects	Concessional loan	Exim Bank
Lagos	n.a.	October 2007	West Africa infrastructure financing mechanism through United Bank of Africa, via a line of credit from Commercial Bank of China		Commercial Bank of China

(continued)

Appendix 3. A Partial Listing of China's Investment in Africa (continued)

Country	Amount (dollars)	Date	Project	Terms and conditions	Financier
Mozambique	2.6 billion	MOU signed April 2006	Mepanda Nkua dam, hydroelectric station, and transmission line; construction of Moamba-Major dam		
Namibia	250 million	Offered February 2007	Loan goes toward paying a Chinese software company to install an electronic management system for public service	Approximately $145 million three-year concessional loan; $100 million credit line	
Namibia	31 million	Signed November 2005	Rehabilitation of railway lines; railway equipment purchase project	Concessional loan	
Nigeria	200 million	Agreement signed January 2006	Communications satellite		Exim Bank (buyers credit)
Nigeria	700 million	Agreement signed May 2005	Construction of two power plants (Papalanto and Omotosho)	Repayment in oil over a twelve-year period	Exim Bank
Nigeria	23 million	Announced November 2005	Finance expansion of Starcomms Ltd., telecom provider	Finance infrastructure projects by public or private sector	Exim Bank
Nigeria	40 billion–50 billion	MOU signed March 2008	Second phase of ICT infrastructure development (connecting rural communities)		SINOSURE (Export Credit Guarantee Agency)
Nigeria	300 million	MOU signed April 2006	Loan for infrastructure projects		
Nigeria	2.5 billion	Announced April 2008		Offered during talks about energy exploration rights	
Nigeria	2.5 billion	Offered 2006; unclear if Nigerian Senate approved request to access facility	Construction of phase 1 of hydro-electric plant; phase 1 railway construction; phase 2 rural telephony	Concessional loan with ten-year tenor	

Country	Amount (US$)	Date	Project	Condition	Financier
DR Congo		Ongoing as of September 2005	Hydro dam at Imboulou; road construction; restoration of Senate building; setting up fixed telephone network		Exim Bank
Rwanda	20 million	Announced summer 2007	Television station and Internet provider		
Sudan	483 million	Letter of intent signed summer 2005	Construction of three electric power stations (one coal in Port Sudan and two gas in El Bagair and Al Fula)		Exim Bank
Sudan	250 million	Project launched in 2003	Merowe hydro dam		Exim Bank, partially
Uganda	106 million	Agreement in spring 2007	Development of ICT system infrastructure		Exim Bank
Zambia		Contracted September 2007	40,000 capacity stadium	Donation by China to Zambia	
Zambia	11 million	2006	Lower Kafue Gorge hydro plant; Fiber-optic network		ZTE Corp.
Zimbabwe	1.3 billion	MOU signed June 2006	Mine coal and build thermal power generators; agreement with China National Construction and Agricultural Machinery Import and Export Corporation (CMAC) and China National Aero-Technology Import and Export Corporation (CATIC)	Chrome mining rights	
Zimbabwe	60 million	Announced June 2006	State radio and television transmission improved in return for chrome	Chrome mining rights	Chinese Development Bank
Zimbabwe	600 million	Signed June 2006	Thermal power station in Sinamatella	Coal mining concession	

Source: Authors' compilation.

DR Congo = Democratic Republic of the Congo; ICT = information and communication technology; MOU = memorandum of understanding; n.a. Not available.

References

Adenikinju, Adeola F. 2005. "African Imperatives in the New World Trade Order: Country Case Study of the Manufacturing Sector in Nigeria." In *Nigeria's Imperatives in the New World Trade Order*, edited by O. E. Ogunkola and A. Bankole. Nairobi and Ibadan: Africa Economic Research Consortium and the Trade Policy Research and Training Programme.

African Development Bank. 2007. *Investing in Africa's Future: The ADB in the 21st Century*. Report of the High Level Panel. Abidjan, Côte d'Ivoire (www.afdb.org/pls/portal/docs/PAGE/ADB_ADMIN_PG/DOCUMENTS/NEWS/HLP%20REPORT-INVESTING%20IN%20AFRICA%E2%80%99S%20FUTURE.PDF).

Amsden, Alice H. 1989. *Asia's Next Giant: South Korea and Late Industrialization*. Oxford University Press.

Asian Development Bank. 2007. "Nam Theun 2 Maintains Momentum." News release (June 6) (www.adb.org/media/Articles/2007/11923-laos-hydroelectrics-projects/).

Ayyagari, Meghana, Asli Demirguc-Kunt, and Vojislav Maksimovic. 2006. "How Important Are Financing Constraints? The Role of Finance in the Business Environment." Policy Research Working Paper 3820. Washington: World Bank.

Bastos, Fabiano, and John Nasir. 2004. "Productivity and the Investment Climate: What Matters Most?" Policy Research Working Paper 3335. Washington: World Bank.

Bates, Robert. 1981. *States and Markets in Tropical Africa: The Political Basis of Agricultural Policy*. 2nd ed. Series on Social Choice and Political Economy. University of California Press.

Biggs, Tyler, Pradeep Srivastava, and Manju Kedia Shah. 1995. "Technological Capabilities and Learning in African Enterprises." RPED Working Paper AFT288. Washington: World Bank, Regional Program on Enterprise Development.

Biggs, Tyler, and Manju Shah. 2006. "African Small and Medium Enterprises, Networks, and Manufacturing Performance." Policy Research Working Paper 3855. Washington: World Bank.

Bigsten, Arne, and others. 2000. "Credit Constraints in Manufacturing Enterprises in Africa." Working Paper 2000.24. Oxford University, Center for the Study of African Economies.

Birdsall, Nancy. 2007. "Do No Harm: Aid, Weak Institutions, and the Missing Middle in Africa." Working Paper 113. Washington: Center for Global Development.

Bratton, Michael, Robert Mattes, and E. Gyimah-Boadi. 2005. *Public Opinion, Democracy, and Market Reform in Africa*. Cambridge University Press.

Bretton Woods Project. 2004. "Acres Debarment: Litmus Test for Bank on Corruption." London (April 5) (www.brettonwoodsproject.org/art.shtml?x=42230).

Burgess, Robin, and Anthony Venables. 2004. "Towards a Microeconomics of Growth." Policy Research Working Paper 3257. Washington: World Bank.

Buys, Piet, Uwe Deichmann, and David Wheeler. 2006. "Road Network Upgrading and Overland Trade Expansion in Sub-Saharan Africa." Policy Research Working Paper 4097. Washington: World Bank.

Buys, Piet, and others. 2007. "Country Stakes in Climate Change Negotiations: Two Dimensions of Vulnerability." Policy Research Working Paper 4300. Washington: World Bank.

Byrd, William, and Alan Gelb. 1990. "Why Industrialize? The Incentives for Rural Community Governments." In *China's Rural Industry: Structure, Development and Reform*, edited by William Byrd and Lin Qingsong. Oxford University Press.

Calderon, Cesar A., and Luis Servén. 2004. "Trends in Infrastructure in Latin America, 1980–2001." Working Paper 269. Santiago: Banco Central de Chile.

Canning, David, and Peter Pedroni. 1999. "Infrastructure and Long Run Economic Growth." Queen's University of Belfast.

Centre for Chinese Studies. 2006. "China's Interest and Activity in Africa's Construction and Infrastructure Sectors: A Research Undertaking Evaluating China's Involvement in Africa's Construction and Infrastructure Sector Prepared for DFID China." South Africa: Stellenbosch University.

Collier, Paul. 2000. "Africa's Comparative Advantage." In *Industrial Development and Policy in Africa*, edited by H. Jalilian, M. Tribe, and J. Weiss. Cheltenham, U.K.: Edward Elgar.

Collier, Paul, and Jan Gunning. 1997. "Explaining African Economic Performance." CSAE Working Paper 97-2.2. Oxford University, Centre for the Study of African Economies.

Demurger, Sylvie. 2001. "Infrastructure Development and Economic Growth: An Explanation for Regional Disparities in China?" *Journal of Comparative Economics* 29, no. 1 (March): 95–117.

Dollar, David, Mary Hallward-Driemeier, and Taye Mengistae. 2005. "Investment Climate and Firm Performance in Developing Economies." *Economic Development and Cultural Change* 54, no. 1 (October): 1–31.

Eifert, Benn, Alan Gelb, and Vijaya Ramachandran. 2005. "Business Environment and Comparative Advantage in Africa: Evidence from the Investment Climate Data." Working Paper 56. Washington: Center for Global Development.

———. 2008 (forthcoming). "The Cost of Doing Business in Africa: Evidence from Enterprise Survey Data." *World Development.*

Emery, James. 2003. "Governance and Private Investment in Africa." In *Beyond Structural Adjustment: The Institutional Context of African Development,* edited by Nicolas van de Walle, Nicole Ball, and Vijaya Ramachandran. New York: Palgrave Macmillan.

Environment News Service. 2003. "Power Giant AES Withdraws from Uganda Dam Project." News release (August 13) (www.ens-newswire.com/ens/aug2003/2003-08-13-02.asp).

Escribano, Alvaro, and J. Luis Guasch. 2005. "Assessing the Impact of the Investment Climate on Productivity Using Firm-Level Data: Methodology and the Cases of Guatemala, Honduras, and Nicaragua." Policy Research Working Paper 3621. Washington: World Bank.

Fafchamps, Marcel. 2004. *Market Institutions in Sub-Saharan Africa: Theory and Evidence.* MIT Press.

Farlam, Peter. 2005. *Working Together: Assessing Public-Private Partnerships in Africa.* Report. NEPAD Policy Focus Series. Johannesburg: South African Institute of International Affairs.

Gelb, Alan, Vijaya Ramachandran, and Ginger Turner. 2007. "Stimulating Growth and Investment in Africa: From Macro to Micro Reforms." *African Development Review* 9, no. 1 (April).

Gelb, Alan, and others. 2007. "What Matters to Businesses? The Relevance of Perceptions Data." Policy Research Working Paper 4446. Washington: World Bank.

Goldstein, Andrea. 2007. "Chinese Contractors in Africa: Insights from a Survey." Presentation in Shanghai, May 16 (www.oecd.org/dataoecd/61/0/39523716.pdf).

Hallward-Driemeier, Mary, Scott Wallsten, and Lixin Colin Xu. 2003. "The Investment Climate and the Firm: Firm-Level Evidence from China." Policy Research Working Paper 3003. Washington: World Bank

Haltiwanger, John, Stefano Scarpetta, and Helena Schweiger. 2006. "Assessing Job Flows across Countries: The Role of Industry, Firm Size, and Regulations." Policy Research Working Paper 4070. Washington: World Bank.

Hausmann, Ricardo, and Andrés Velasco. 2005. "Slow Growth in Latin America: Common Outcomes, Common Causes?" Paper written for seminar "Una nueva agenda de desarrollo económico para América Latina." Salamanca, Spain, October 7–8, 2005. Kennedy School of Government, Harvard University (http://ksghome.harvard.edu/~rhausma/docs/slowgrowth_salamanca_0510.pdf).

Hoff, Karla, and Arijit Sen. 2006. "The Kin System as a Poverty Trap?" Policy Research Paper 3575. World Bank: World Bank.

Honohan, Patrick, and Thorsten Beck. *Making Finance Work for Africa.* Washington: World Bank.

Infrastructure Consortium for Africa (ICA). 2008. "Final Outcome Statement." Paper prepared for the Fourth Annual Meeting of the Infrastructure Consortium for Africa. Tokyo, March 13–14 (www.icafrica.org/fileadmin/documents/Tokyo/Final_Outcome_Statement_ICA_Annual_Meeting_Tokyo.pdf).

Jacobs, G., and A. Aeron-Thomas. 2000. "Africa Road Safety: Review Final Report." Report prepared for U.S. Department of Transportation, Federal Highway Administration (http://safety.fhwa.dot.gov/about/international/africa/africa.htm).

Johnson, Simon, Jonathan D. Ostry, and Arvind Subramanian. 2007. "The Prospects for Sustained Growth in Africa: Benchmarking the Constraints." NBER Working Paper 13120. Cambridge, Mass.: National Bureau of Economic Research.

Kassim, Yang Razali. 2006. "The Shenzhen-Hongkong Model: Singapore and the South Johore Economic Region." IDSS Commentaries 96/2006. Singapore: Institute of Defence and Strategic Studies.

Krugman, Paul. 1980. "Scale Economies, Product Differentiation, and the Pattern of Trade." *American Economic Review* 70, no. 5: 950–59.

———.1991a. *Geography and Trade*. MIT Press

———.1991b. "Increasing Returns and Economic Geography." *Journal of Political Economy* 99, no. 3: 483–99.

Lall, Somik, and Taye Mengistae. 2005a. "The Impact of Business Environment and Economic Geography on Plant Level Productivity: An Analysis of Industry." Policy Research Working Paper 3664. Washington: World Bank (July).

———. 2005b. "Business Environment, Clustering and Industry Location: Evidence from Indian Cities." Policy Research Working Paper 3675. Washington: World Bank (August).

Limao, Nuno, and Anthony J. Venables. 1999. "Infrastructure, geographical disadvantage, and transport costs," Policy Research Working Paper 2257. Washington: World Bank.

Mazumdar, Dipak and Ata Mazaheri. 2003. *The African Manufacturing Firm: An Analysis Based on Firms in Sub-Saharan Africa*. London: Routledge.

Mengistae, Taye. 2001. "Indigenous Ethnicity and Entrepreneurial Success in Africa: Some Evidence from Ethiopia." Policy Research Working Paper 2534. Washington: World Bank.

Moss, Todd. 2007. *African Development: Making Sense of the Issues and Actors*. Boulder, Colo: Lynne Rienner.

Moss, Todd, and Sarah Rose. 2006. "The Investment Climate Facility for Africa: Does it Deserve U.S. Support?" *CGD Notes* (August). Washington: Center for Global Development.

Munnell, Alicia H. 1992. "Infrastructure Investment and Economic Growth." *Journal of Economic Perspectives* 6, no. 4 (Fall): 189–98.

Ndulu Benno, and Stephen A. O'Connell. 2006. "Policy Plus: African Growth Performance 1960–2000." Draft chapter 1 of the synthesis volume of the AERC's collaborative research project: *Explaining African Economic Growth*. Nairobi, Kenya: African Economic Research Consortium.

Organization for Economic Cooperation and Development (OECD). 2003/2004. *African Economic Outlook 2003/2004*. Paris: African Development Bank and OECD.

Platteau, Jean-Philippe, and Yujiro Hayami. 1998. "Resource Endowments and Agricultural Development: Africa versus Asia." In *The Institutional Foundations of East Asian Economic Development*, edited by Yujiro Hayami and Masahiko Aoki, pp. 357–410. Proceedings of the IEA conference held in Tokyo, Japan. Houndmills, Basingstoke: Macmillan.

Power Planning Associates. 2007. "Bujagali II—Economic and Financial Evaluation Study: Final Report." Report prepared for the International Finance Corporation. Washington.

Radelet, Steve. 2008. "Economic Growth in the Emerging Democracies of Africa." Presented at the NBER Africa Project Conference, February 2008 (www.nber.org).

Ramachandran, Vijaya, Manju Kedia Shah, and Gaiv Tata. 2007. "Does Influence Peddling Impact Industrial Competition? Evidence from the Africa Investment Climate Surveys." CGD Working Paper 127. Washington: Center for Global Development.

Raturi, Mayank, and Anand V. Swamy. 1999. "Explaining Ethnic Differentials in Credit Market Outcomes in Zimbabwe." *Economic Development and Cultural Change* 47, no. 3 (April): 585–604.

Reinikka, Ritva, and Jakob Svensson. 2006. "Using Micro-Surveys to Measure and Explain Corruption." *World Development* 34 no. 2 (February): 359–70.

Shaw, Angus. 2008. "Power Outages in Zambia, Zimbabwe." Associated Press, January 20.

Soderbom, Mans, and Francis Teal. 2003. "Are Manufactured Exports the Key to Economic Success in Africa?" *Journal of African Economies* 12, no. 1 (March): 1–29.

Stead, Steve. 2007. "The Malaysian Success Story: Lessons for South Africa?" Brenthurst Discussion Paper 10/2007. Johannesburg, South Africa: Brenthurst Foundation.

Tangri, Roger. 1999. *The Politics of Patronage in Africa*. Trenton, N.J.: Africa World Press.

Teal, Francis. 1998. "The Ghanaian Manufacturing Sector 1991–95: Firm Growth, Productivity and Convergence." CSAE Working Paper 98/17. Oxford University, Centre for the Study of African Economies (June).

Television Trust for the Environment. 2002. "Stream Line, Kenya." London (www.tve.org/ho/doc.cfm?aid=871).

Van de Walle, Nicolas. 2001. *African Economies and the Politics of Permanent Crisis, 1979–1999*. Cambridge University Press.

Wheeler, David. 2008. "Crossroads at Mmamabula: Will the World Bank Choose the Clean Energy Path?" Working Paper 140. Washington: Center for Global Development (www.cgdev.org/content/publications/detail/15401).

Wines, Michael. 2007. "Toiling in the Dark: Africa's Power Crisis." *New York Times*, July 29.

Wood, Adrian, and Jörg Mayer. 1998. "Africa's Export Structure in a Comparative Perspective." Geneva, Switzerland: UN Conference on Trade and Development (UNCTAD) and University of Oxford (October) (http://ssrn.com/abstract =141202).

World Bank. 2000. *Can Africa Claim the 21st Century?* edited by Alan H. Gelb. Oxford University Press.

————. 2001–06. *Investment Climate Assessment.* Various countries. Washington: Regional Program on Enterprise Development, Africa Private Sector Group (www1. worldbank.org/rped/index.asp?page=icas) and (www.worldbank. org/rped).

————. 2006a. "Technical and Economic Assessment of Off-grid, Mini-grid and Grid Electrification." Technologies. Summary Report. Washington.

————. 2006b. "World Bank Sanctions Lahmeyer International for Corrupt Activities in Bank-Financed Projects." Press release. Washington (November 6).

————. 2001–07. *Doing Business.* Survey data and reports (www.doingbusiness.org/).

————. 2007. *World Development Indicators* (WDI). CD-ROM database. Washington.

Zoellick. 2008. "A Challenge of Economic Statecraft." Speech sponsored by the Center for Global Development. Washington, April 2 (http://go.worldbank.org/ KRFPZ4OU30).

Index